ERNST TOCH

THE SHAPING FORCES IN MUSIC

An Inquiry into the Nature of
Harmony · Melody · Coun

With a New Introduction by
LAWRENCE WESCHLER

And a New Complete Checklist of Toch's Works

DOVER PUBLICATIONS, INC., NEW YORK

Published in Canada by General Publishing Company, Ltd., 30 Lesmill Road, Don Mills, Toronto, Ontario.
Published in the United Kingdom by Constable and Company, Ltd.

This Dover edition, first published in 1977, is an unabridged republication of the work originally published by Criterion Music Corp., N.Y., in 1948. Criterion Music Corp. continues to distribute the clothbound edition.

New in the present paperbound edition are the Introduction by Lawrence Weschler, the checklist of Toch's works and the translation of the hitherto unpublished letter from Thomas Mann to Ernst Toch. A few obvious typographical errors have been corrected.

The publisher is grateful to Mr. Michael Mann and to the S. Fischer Verlag, Frankfurt am Main, for permission to print the Thomas Mann letter.

International Standard Book Number: 0-486-23346-4
Library of Congress Catalog Card Number: 76-9950

Manufactured in the United States of America
Dover Publications, Inc.
180 Varick Street
New York, N.Y. 10014

INTRODUCTION
TO THE DOVER EDITION

*I believe that we can only be the product of a long line of
ancestors and that each creating artist, involuntarily, is
placed as a link in this chain. He cooperates on the con-
tinuity to the degree in which the timeless is more important
than the timebound.*

ERNST TOCH

Ernst Toch was born in Vienna on December 7, 1887, into
the family of Moritz Toch, a humble Jewish dealer in unpro-
cessed leather. The Toch family had only just attained a relative
financial security with the generation of Moritz, and the father
assumed that Ernst, his only son, would eventually take on the
family business. There was no musical background or encouragement for the young boy, and, in later years when his interest in
music became more acute, Ernst even faced considerable opposition from his parents and was forced to pursue his investigations
in secret.

From the very start, nevertheless, this precocious child
developed a fanatic interest in the universe of sounds; it was
perhaps only natural that in Vienna, a city so deeply engrossed
in its rich heritage, such an interest soon concentrated on music.
In his first encounter with a piano, in the darkened back room of
his grandmother's pawnshop, the young boy intuited complex
melodies. A few months later, the brief tenancy in the Toch
household of an amateur violinist allowed the boy his first
acquaintance with sheet music; after a few evenings of rapt
curiosity, young Toch had puzzled out the fundamentals of
musical notation.

In later years, Toch would characterize the epiphany of
musical talent in such a culturally desolate family setting as a
miracle; and, indeed, the genesis of Toch's creative genius affords
few parallels in the history of music.

This Introduction is a slightly modified version of the October 1974
booklet *Ernst Toch, 1887–1964; A biographical essay ten years after his
passing*, a publication of the Ernst Toch Archive of the UCLA Music Library.
Mr. Weschler is co-director of the Archive.

Notes which Toch drafted in preparation for an interview, during the last year of his life, include the following remembrance of his unique apprenticeship in musical theory and composition:

> I have not studied with anybody . . . I was left on my own and managed to acquire at length what I learned in a completely autodidactic way . . . I made the decisive discovery that pocket scores existed. The quartet I happened to see in the window of a music shop was one of the so-called ten famous quartets of Mozart. I bought it. I was carried away when reading this score. Perhaps in order to prolong my exaltation, I started to copy it, which gave me deeper insight. By and by, I bought and copied all the ten scores. But I did not stop at that. After having copied three or four I became aware of the structure of the single movements. And when I started to copy the fifth, I decided I would only continue with my copying up to the repeat sign, and then try my hand at making that part myself which leads back to the original key (called "development" as I was later informed). Then I compared with the original. I felt crushed. Was I a flea, a mouse, a little nothing when I compared what I did with what Mozart did; but still I did not give up and continued my strange method to grope along in this way and to force Mozart to correct me. And he not only replaced for me every living teacher but outdid them all.

The unusual circumstances of this education no doubt account, in part, for the special reverence with which, throughout his life, Toch would honor Mozart and the other great masters of the Tradition.

"At the same time," Toch's notes continue, "the irrepressible urge to write string quartets entirely of my own arose and possessed me." By age seventeen, Toch had already composed six quartets, along with several other chamber pieces, always in secret, each work displaying a more sophisticated grasp of the composer's craft. One day in 1905, Joseph Fuchs, Toch's schoolmate, noticed him scribbling furiously under his desk and inquired after the object of such absorbed attention. Informed that these were the final touches of a string quartet, Fuchs asked to borrow the score. A week later Toch received a postcard from Arnold Rosé, the first violinist of the renowned Rosé Quartet, notifying him that his new *Quartet*, opus 12, had been accepted for performance.

Despite a few early successes of this kind, Toch's vocation seemed to be in serious jeopardy as he completed his secondary schooling. Continually insecure as to the quality of his ill-begotten talents, Toch saw little hope of any livelihood deriving from his eccentric hobby. And so, somewhat forlorn, he enrolled at the University of Vienna to begin working toward a medical degree.

Suddenly, in 1909, it was announced that Toch had won the Mozart Prize, the coveted award of a quadrennial international competition for young composers which he had entered three years earlier on a lark. The prize included a four-year stipend, with a one-year fellowship to the Frankfurt Conservatory. Elated, Toch journeyed to Frankfurt and reported to the head of the composition department, Iwan Knorr, eager for his first official lesson. "You wanted to study with me?" stammered Knorr. "But I was going to ask if you would allow me to study with you." And indeed, Toch had already reached full maturity as a composer. His dynamic *String Quartet*, opus 18, composed shortly after his arrival in Frankfurt, exhibited a masterly control and range.

Toch thereafter remained in Germany, a land already vibrant with anticipation of one of the great creative upsurges in the history of music. Toch was appointed professor of composition at the Mannheim Hochschule für Musik, and through a steady stream of impressive new works, notably, the *Violin Sonata*, opus 21 (1912), he generated a growing reputation as an important heir to the late Romantic tradition of Brahms.

With the coming of the war in 1914, however, Toch fell silent. Drafted into the Austrian infantry, he was assigned to the front lines in the Italian Alps, where his early military enthusiasm eroded into despair. The numbing tension of battle nearly stilled his creative drive, the only exception being the pastoral *Spitzweg Serenade*, opus 25, a trio for strings actually composed in the trenches. It was during the Vienna furloughs of these years that Toch's long courtship of Lilly Zwack, the cultured daughter of a Jewish banker, intensified and culminated in marriage (1916). Soon thereafter, following the intercession of a committee of concerned musicians, Toch was transferred behind the lines to the destitute back-country of Galicia, where he remained until the Armistice. Upon the conclusion of hostilities, Toch quickly returned to Mannheim.

As Toch's creative energies resurfaced, it became clear that his five years of silence had veiled a profound inner transformation. His new *String Quartet,* opus 26 (1919), scandalized the audience at its Mannheim premiere. Toch quickly soared to the vanguard of the *Neue Musik* movement which was about to electrify Central Europe. Years later Toch recalled some of the forces behind the modernist revolution:

> The musical revolution did not come about suddenly: gradually composers began to feel that the old idiom of tonality had exhausted itself and was incapable of utterance without repeating itself, that the once live and effective tensions of its harmonic scope were worn out and had lost their effect. Inevitable at the same time was a strong reaction against over-emotional musical expression, epitomized particularly in the works of Richard Wagner . . . Indeed, it was refreshing, an inner need, to get away from the over-emotional type of music which was so characteristic of the latter half of the nineteenth century. It was as refreshing as a plunge into cold water on a tropical summer day.

And yet Toch played down the significance of the "New" in the modernist upsurge. He insisted that

> The differences at the time they occur are at first very noticeable, and even aggressive. After ten years they are hardly perceptible; after a hundred years they are of interest only to the research specialist. What then remains or is doomed to disappear, that alone decides their worth or lack of worth.

The next fifteen years comprised one of the most prolific phases of Toch's lifework; they likewise became the years of his greatest public renown. In 1923, following a series of stirring successes, B. Schott's Söhne, the venerable Mainz publishing firm, signed the young composer to a ten-year contract which would guarantee him a forum for his new work and the steady income with which to pursue it. Toch celebrated the contract by composing his *Burlesken* for piano, opus 31, whose lively third movement, "The Juggler," became an instant sensation and remains a modern classic.

Although, in the years before the War, Toch honed his craft through concentration on chamber works (and he was to continue to favor the string quartet with three new compositions between 1919 and 1924), the twenties were to witness the expansion of his range into all musical forms. In particular, Toch turned increasingly toward orchestral compositions, culminating in 1925 with the *Cello Concerto*, opus 35, followed in 1926 by the *Piano Concerto*, opus 38. The latter work, premiered by Walter Gieseking, required more than twenty full-orchestra rehearsals before its sensational performance a few months later at the 1927 Frankfurt International Music Festival, with Walter Frey as soloist and Hermann Scherchen conducting. Its enthusiastic reception by audience and critics alike secured Toch's reputation as one of the foremost composers in Germany.

Toch then turned his attention to the operatic stage and composed his popular *The Princess and the Pea*, opus 43, soon followed by the charmingly mischievous chamber opera, *Edgar and Emily*, opus 46, based on an ingenious libretto by Christian Morgenstern.

By 1928 Toch had moved from Mannheim to Berlin, the center of creative excitement in all of the arts, and here he became increasingly interested in cooperative ventures, especially in composing incidental music for the Berlin stage (the tender "Idyll" in the *Divertimento for Wind Orchestra*, opus 39, for example, was originally conceived as a pastoral interlude for an expressionist production of Euripides' *Bacchae*). Toch also attracted considerable attention through his puckish enthusiasm for instrumental experimentation, as in a sequence of complex works which he scored for mechanical piano. But his most popular innovation came in 1930 with his famous musical joke, the *Geographical Fugue for Speaking Chorus*, in which he patterned a sequence of rhythmic place-names into a formal fugue. Years later, in 1961, Toch would revive the genre in his *Valse*, arranging the clichés of cocktail party banter into 3/4 time.

So famous had Toch become by 1932 that he was invited to be the first (and last) German composer to tour the United States under the auspices of the remarkable Pro Musica Society. Although Toch was deeply impressed by the vibrancy of American life, and became especially enamored of Southern California, he was somewhat bemused by the provincial musical sensibilities of

many of his American audiences. Among his notes for an introductory lecture to one Pro Musica concert, we find a passage in
which he tried to coax his American listeners into a more recep-
tive attitude *vis à vis* the modernist trends in Europe:

> You must listen without always wanting to compare with the
> musical basis you already have. You must imagine that you inherited
> from your ancestors different compartments in the musical part of
> your brain, just as you inherited any other physical or intellectual
> qualities. Now when you hear a piece from the pre-classic, classic,
> or romantic periods, the sounds fall without any trouble and agree-
> ably into the already prepared compartments. But when music for
> which you have no prepared compartments strikes your ear, what
> happens? Either the music remains outside you or you force it with
> all your might into one of these compartments, although it does
> not fit. The compartment is either too long or too short, either too
> narrow or too wide, and that hurts you and you blame the music.
> But in reality you are to blame, because you force it into a com-
> partment into which it does not fit, instead of calmly, passively,
> quietly, and without opposition, helping the music to build a new
> compartment for itself.

Toch's American tour in 1932 was already haunted by the
darkening shadow of the Nazi presence in Germany. After his
return to Berlin, during the few months remaining before Hitler's
final seizure of power, Toch worked intensely on a *Second Piano
Concerto*, opus 61, which was to have its premiere disrupted by
brownshirts and its publication canceled by a suddenly "anti-
Bolshevik" Schott publishing house. Early in 1933 Toch resolved
to flee Germany.

For purposes of his escape Toch profited from his long-
scheduled selection (together with Richard Strauss) to represent
Germany at a musicological convention in Florence in April,
1933. Toch never returned to Berlin, fleeing instead to France.
After he had established himself in a Paris hotel, Toch tele-
graphed his wife a revealingly coded "all-clear" signal: it read,
simply, "I have my pencil."

He had little else. His publisher had abandoned him, his
music was being burned, the plates broken. Concerts of his works
were canceled; the only traces remaining in Germany of his once

vibrant reputation were the doctored photographs gracing the occasional exhibitions of "degenerate music." And it would be several years before he would even find a new home. Paris, suddenly swollen with German exiles, offered little refuge, and the Toch family soon moved on to London. Toch remained in England for one year, but here, likewise, work permits were in short supply, and the family caromed on to New York. While on the boʔ to America, Toch composed his lyrically melancholy *Big Ben Variations*, opus 62, a tone poem evoking the Westminster Chimes as they sounded one foggy midnight to a departing wanderer.

Like many German exiles, Toch accepted a professorship at the New School for Social Research. Although he stayed in New York for two years, Toch never quite acclimatized himself to the concrete and traffic of Manhattan. In 1936, partly at the instigation of his new American friend, George Gershwin, Toch was commissioned by Warner Bros. to score a film, and by mid-year he had established residence in Pacific Palisades. During the next ten years Toch would frequently supplement his meager royalties through studio work. Owing to the "eeriness" of his modernist idiom, Toch was quickly typecast as a specialist in horror and chase scenes, and he was to have a hand in most of the mysteries coming out of the Paramount studios for the next several years. During the next decade his scores would receive three Academy Award nominations.

That Toch felt he had at last found a permanent home in the ocean canyons of Southern California is clear from the sudden renewal of his fading creative drive. In rapid succession Toch produced two of his most powerful and striking chamber works, the *String Trio*, opus 63, and the *Piano Quintet*, opus 64. These two complex and demanding works represent the culmination of the mature style of Toch's German years. And yet they fell on deaf ears in the America of the thirties, generating few performances and indeed remaining unpublished until 1946. This unresponsiveness of American audiences to the modernist style is surely one reason (the osmosis of Hollywood film scoring may be another) for the slow bending of Toch's creative production during the late thirties and forties into a more harmonic and tonal idiom, such as that employed in Toch's next composition, the *Cantata of the Bitter Herbs*, opus 65.

In December 1937 Toch received news of the death of his mother in Vienna. While attending the ritual prayers for the dead at a local synagogue, Toch conceived the project of a cantata based on the *Haggada*, the scripture traditionally read at the family table at Passover, commemorating the Exodus of the Jews from Egypt. Although by no means an Orthodox Jew, Toch perceived a universal human significance in the Passover tale of liberation from the yoke of oppression. But of course this eternal message bore a particular urgency during those horrible months: while Toch was composing the haunting chorus, based on the psalmist's text, "When Adonoy brought back his sons from Zion, it would be like a dream . . .," Hitler's armies invaded Austria and sealed Vienna, the town of his birth.

The Nazi invasion was to initiate a vertiginous period of depression in Toch's life. Gnawing anxieties about the fate of trapped friends and relatives (Toch had more than sixty cousins still in Austria) were sublimated into time-consuming negotiations with international bureaucracies in desperate, often futile, attempts to gain their freedom. Meanwhile, the financial pressure of temporarily sponsoring a burgeoning family of dispossessed exiles forced Toch to channel ever-larger portions of his creative life into more lucrative employment. Thus, Toch found himself devoting long hours to film work; his early enthusiasm for the artistic cross-fertilization possible in film gradually soured into bitter disillusionment with the insensitivity of the studio heads, and he came to despise the necessary prostitution of his talents. Meanwhile, the hours outside the studio were increasingly devoted to teaching, at first privately, and then, after 1940, at the University of Southern California as well. By report of his students, Toch was an exceptionally sensitive and effective teacher (perhaps due to the unique genesis of his own vocation, Toch was able to catalyze in others a similarly organic and intuitive apprenticeship in the craft of composition) ; but it was precisely through this high level of commitment that teaching, even more than studio work, sapped Toch's energies to exhaustion.

With his hours thus gerrymandered in extraneous pursuits, Toch had decreasing time to devote purely to his own work. Furthermore, the loss of a responsive audience (a situation magnified by labyrinthine difficulties with his American publishers) rendered hollow the few hours he was able to preserve for his creative life. Thus in 1943 he complained to a friend:

> For quite some time I am not in a very happy frame of mind. Disappointments and sorrows render me frustrated and lonesome. I become somehow reluctant to go on writing if my work remains more or less paper in desks and on shelves.

Underlying all of Toch's anxieties was the fear that he had irrevocably squandered his musical vocation, that he had lost everything—even, in effect, his pencil. Indeed, these years were parched by the most harrowing dry spell of Toch's life. While between 1919 and 1933 Toch had created more than 35 works, during the obverse years from 1933 to 1947 Toch struggled to conceive eight, with barely a single work between 1938 and 1945.

And yet somehow, perhaps tapping some primal source available only to one brought so low, Toch was on the verge of a stupendous regeneration. In the final months of the war, Toch's letters tentatively explored the image of the rainbow, metaphor for renewal. For his own renewal, Toch returned to the most fundamental of his forms, the string quartet. "As for me," he exuberantly wrote a friend, "I am in the midst of writing a string quartet, the first of its kind after 18 years. Writing a string quartet was a sublime delight before the world knew of the atomic bomb, and—in this respect, it has not changed—it still is." The *Quartet*, opus 70 (1946), bore as motto the lines of a poem by Eduard Mörike: "I do not know what it is I mourn for—it is unknown sorrow; only through my tears can I see the beloved light of the sun."

Toch was simultaneously completing work on his book, *The Shaping Forces in Music*, the research for which had increasingly possessed him. During the early forties Toch had been startled by the lack of an appropriate textbook for use in his classes, one whose theories could integrate both the modern and the classical styles. With this in mind he undertook his own survey of the musical literature. Writing one friend, he reported,

> I never expected so much fascination to come from investigations on the nature of musical theory and composition. Aspects unfolding to me show why the rules of established musical theories could not be applied to "modern" music, why there seemed to be a break all along the line, either discrediting our contemporary work or everything that has been derived from the past. To my amazement I find that those theories are only false with reference to contemporary music because they are just as false with reference to the old music, from which they have been deduced; and that in correcting them to precision you get the whole immense structure of music into your focus.

Thus Toch's creative regeneration in the late forties recapitulated the originary apprenticeship of his childhood: once again, through an exploration of the masters, Toch recovered the essential stream of his own vocation.

The years immediately following the War, paradoxically, were to prove the most difficult of all, for now the dense pattern of extraneous obligations threatened to strangle the tentative budding of his renewed vocation. Torn by these conflicting pressures, Toch was felled by a major heart attack in the autumn of 1948.

"I am plowing through a dark and stormy sea," Toch wrote a friend from his sickbed. But within a few weeks he would deem this seizure one of the most fortunate events of his life. Suddenly, years of sedimented obligations fell away, and he was forced to partake of the calm he so desperately needed. Years of stymied meditations seemed to rush to the surface of his consciousness; he experienced these months as an overwhelming "religious epiphany." A few years later, in his essay "What Is Good Music?," Toch would suggest:

> Nearness to life, nearness to nature and humanity—who has it? I think the one who contains in himself an irrational, unconquerable bastion, untouched, for which I have no other word but *religiousness*. To be sure, this quality does not refer to any specific creed. . . . It has nothing to do with a man's interests and activities, nothing

to do even with the conduct of a man's life. The word "religion" derives from the Latin "religare"—to tie, to tie fast, to tie back. Tie what to what? Tie man to the oneness of the Universe, to the creation of which he feels himself a part, to the will that willed his existence, to the law he can only divine. It is a fundamental human experience, dim in some, shining in others, rare in some, frequent in others, conscious in some, unconscious in others. But there is no great creation in either art or science which is not ultimately rooted in this climate of the soul, whatever the means of translation and substantiation.

In terms of the dialectic between technique and inspiration which Toch increasingly favored in his later writings, it was clear that his dry years resulted from an atrophy of the spiritual dimension, and it was precisely that dimension which was being replenished in the months following Toch's brush with death. Toch began work on his *First Symphony*.

As soon as he had recovered sufficiently to travel, Toch returned to Vienna, the city of his childhood, there to complete and unveil the work which was a signal of a new beginning. This *First Symphony*, dedicated to his childhood friend and secret promoter, Joseph Fuchs, would in time be followed by six others. Such a complete flowering of the symphonic form so late in a composer's life was unprecedented in the history of music.

The first three of these symphonies should be interpreted as a musical triptych, the sustained outpouring of a single source in Toch's deeply religious and humanistic experience of the late forties. Of one of these symphonies, Toch wrote a friend:

> I had meant to call one movement "the Song of the Heritage"; I refrained from it in order not to appear too "literary." However, the feeling reverberates more or less in all of my present writing, a kind of deep-rooted link between a far past and a far future, and it fills me with great humility and great awe (I mean to be able to be the mouthpiece of such experience).

The *First Symphony*, opus 72 (1949-50), bore a motto from Luther, "Although the world with devils filled should threaten to undo us, we will not fear, for God has willed his truth to triumph through us." The *Second Symphony*, opus 73 (1953), dedicated to Albert Schweitzer, a man whom Toch revered (he would insist that the symphony was not only dedicated to Schweitzer but "dictated" by him), carried the Biblical motto from Jacob's wrestling with the Angel, "I shall not let thee go except thou bless me." And finally, the *Third Symphony*, opus 75 (1954-55), perhaps the finest of them all, bore lines from Goethe's *The Sorrows of Young Werther*, "Indeed I am a wanderer, a pilgrim on the earth—but what else are you?" Toch would sometimes refer to this work as his "musical autobiography," and a sensitive listening suggests many motifs drawn from Toch's own life experience (for example, in the first movement, the military cadences joyously entering and then splintering in tragedy); but just as the motto implicates its reader, so in this symphony autobiography suggests the microcosm of universal human history. Soon after its premiere by William Steinberg, this symphony was awarded the Pulitzer Prize.

Toch's creative production would now continue unabated until his death. Restlessly wandering in search of the peace necessary for his composing, Toch divided his last years between Santa Monica, Zurich, and his favorite refuge at the MacDowell Colony in New Hampshire. In one of his most prolific phases, Toch would move during his last fifteen years from opus 71 to opus 98, including the seven symphonies and a final opera, *The Last Tale*, opus 88 (1960-62), which Toch considered his greatest work (although it has yet to see its premiere).

The dramatic, almost epic, scope of the first three symphonies would be echoed in some of the later works, such as *Jephta (The Fifth Symphony)*, opus 89, in 1961. But Toch's later works generally sounded a more lyrical, and often melancholy, tone, such as that of the pensive *Notturno*, opus 77 (a nostalgic fantasy born of an evening walk in the woods of the MacDowell Colony in 1953), or the poignant *Fourth Symphony*, opus 80 (a 1957 memorial for the Colony's founder, Mrs. Miriam MacDowell).

During those final years Toch worked at a furious pace, haunted by the specter of the time already lost, overflowing with musical ideas he feared he might never complete. "Never in my life has writing come as easily to me as it does now," he told one friend. "I am writing myself empty," he confided to another. But, although the last works were composed with an almost Faustian intensity, they breathe a serene, sometimes almost elfin, leisure and calm. While the compositions between 1947 and 1955 seemed to derive power from their homage to the Tradition, the works after 1955 tended toward an increasingly personal, almost introverted, idiom. He abandoned many of the classical forms and seemed to disdain rigid architectonics in favor of what appear almost roving fantasies. Often in the final two symphonies and the two sinfoniettas (opuses 93, 95, 96, and 97, all composed during his last year), the lyric line breaks free of all restrictions. The orchestration becomes leaner and clearer, partly perhaps because of the pressure of the relentless passage of time.

In early September, 1964, Toch was suddenly hospitalized in Los Angeles; he was dying of stomach cancer. In a last note to his wife, he apologized for the eccentricities and inconveniences of years in service of the muse, but, he concluded,

> Ich treibe nicht, ich werde getrieben
> Ich schreibe nicht, ich werde geschrieben
>
> I do not press, I am pressed;
> I do not write, I am written.

Ernst Toch died on October 1, 1964. The scribbled pages found by his bedside contained the early drafts of a new string quartet.

During his last years, Toch would sometimes refer to himself wistfully as "the world's most forgotten composer," and his melancholy joke betrayed a painful validity. But if Toch's music seemed in temporary eclipse, this was in part because of the integrity and independence of a lonely artist, leader or follower of no school, who insisted on striking the proper balance between innovation and tradition, and hence found himself dismissed simultaneously as too old-fashioned by the avant-garde and too modern by the traditionalists. But with the passage of time these artificial distinctions are beginning to fade, and Toch's oeuvre is being reassessed in terms he would have preferred, as a single link in the long chain of the musical tradition. And as such, Toch's music is prized for the mastery of its craftsmanship and the depth of its inspiration.

LAWRENCE WESCHLER

To the country which gave me shelter when shelter was taken from me I dedicate this book in everlasting gratitude.

I do not know—no composer does—by whom my music is going to be liked, by whom disliked, by whom met with indifference. But having lived here long enough to know my fellow citizens' hunger both for music and education I may perhaps hope that this book will reach and help also some of those whom my music will not reach or affect.

I wish I could convey that this dedication is not a mere gesture. Life and work were put back into my hands when they were doomed for me to cease. With this awareness, and with the awareness also that whatever I have created since then and may still create is rightfully this country's, I presume to offer this dedication. May the book return in humble service and usefulness a fraction of what I have received.

E. T.

LETTER FROM THOMAS MANN
TO ERNST TOCH

Toward the beginning of 1948, while the original edition of *The Shaping Forces in Music* was in preparation, Toch asked Mann to write a foreword. In the following letter (translated from the German), which has never been published before, Mann explained why he could not comply with the request. Now (1976) that the interval of years has done away with the painful scruples of the passing moment, it seems ironically just that the letter of refusal should serve as a foreword, and a most satisfactory one, to Toch's book.

16 Jan. 1948

Dear Dr. Toch,

If I must tell you that I cannot grant your and your publisher's wish, it is certainly *not* the result of my reading your book, in which I was engrossed very intensively in the last few days. On the contrary, encouragement is so much the basic quality of this excellent treatise that it could even encourage me to write an introduction to it, and it is very distressing indeed to be denied the use of one's courage.

Beyond any question, it is the most amiable book of instruction and perception in the field of music that has ever come to my knowledge—lucid, clever, simple, cheerful and comforting; endowed with a liberality that dispels superstition and false pomp; broad-minded,[1] benevolently progressive, yes, optimistic in matters of the future of Occidental music and the many possibilities still open to it; not discussing problems from the outside but elucidating them from within, in an actually entertaining fashion; simplifying and at the same time enlivening; *productive* as I have rarely, or never, found a theoretical work, because what it gives is, basically, not theory but the encouragingly practical findings of a creative artist. And so on. I tell this to you, I am going to tell it to others, and I have already told it to several people.

However, I cannot make it into a foreword. That I cannot pass myself off as a musical expert, right after my last novel[2] has displayed, in a somewhat swindling way, a little musical knowledge acquired ad hoc, is the smallest point.

I feel ashamed to mention the urgency of my own affairs, yet they are claiming my attention; I am not the master of my own time. The English translation of the above-mentioned novel is due to arrive; I expect the manuscript any day; I must endure the tortures of going through it; I must correspond with the equally suffering lady[3] ("I am committing a murder!") in order to fight over details. Knopf is preparing a one-volume monumental edition of the Joseph tetralogy and is asking me to do a foreword for that enormous accomplishment in book production—that foreword I will have to write by all means. I have a great deal to write and dictate in connection with the publication of the new novel in Europe. A new work, not voluminous but daring as we cannot help being daring, is in preparation—is prepared—and I am dying to *start* it somehow or other, whether "plunging medias in res" or "starting from afar,"[4] I do not know yet; perhaps I will begin at the end and then start from the beginning.

There is another thing. The writing of a foreword for you would expose me to all possible further demands of this kind; it would expose me also to many people whom I have already refused. But the matter is more ticklish and personal. [A relative] is also writing a book on music theory—not as good and happy, I am afraid, as yours but grounded more on combativeness and pugnaciously intellectual, I am *afraid* (this is between ourselves). And yet—why for *you* and not for *him*, since he would need it so much more? It is obvious and unpleasant. I have to take it into account.

There you have my position. It is almost as difficult as the situation of music, which, as I feel, your book has alleviated and freed from gloom in a fashion most deserving of thanks—although you failed to do anything for *my* situation. But what I want to emphasize especially is that you certainly made no mistake nor acted wrongly in approaching me. On the contrary, I agree—and I do not believe that I am making an arrogant statement—that your idea was *correct* in itself. Only the circumstances are adverse to it, as is the surety that if I complied with your idea, three months from now [my relative] would give me a manuscript on the philosophy of music to read with a certain purpose in mind.

And yet I could hardly say to whom else you could have seriously applied. Best of all, to no one! I do *not* agree that a foreword by a second party is necessary or even desirable. Believe me—and your publisher should believe it, too—your book speaks for itself. At the very first glance, there is nothing fear-inspiring in it;

in fact, it possesses a particular clarity, accessibility, perspicuity; and wherever one opens it, one sees at once what it wants to express, what sort of mind created it. Besides, you have said it yourself in the preface.

Much worse off in this respect—I mean, as regards friendly accessibility, perspicuity, sense of proportion—is the book that I am sending you together with this letter—the novel I have mentioned several times. I did not intend to burden you with it, but now I find that the gift is appropriate and that the volume belongs in your hands. I trust that the sympathy with the fate of music to which the thing at least testifies will allow you to pardon many a passage in it objectionable to the expert.

Yours sincerely,
Thomas Mann

1 This word is in English in the original.

2 *Doctor Faustus.*

3 H. T. Lowe-Porter, the translator of *Doctor Faustus* and many other books by Mann. The exclamation in parentheses is in English in the original.

4 The two phrases in quotation marks are in English in the original.

The copy of *Doctor Faustus* that accompanied the letter bore the following inscription (translated from the German) :

To Ernst Toch,
who does not need the Devil.
With neighborly greetings,

Thomas Mann

Pacific Palisades
16 Jan. 1948

Both the letter and the book are in the Ernst Toch Archive in the Music Library of the University of California, Los Angeles.

PREFACE

This book contains a compilation of observations and ideas which have accumulated through years of experience as a composer and teacher.

It attempts to bring out and emphasize the timeless and permanent features of music as against the time-bound and transient ones. In doing so it attempts to reconcile the at-times-"classical" with the at-times-"modern."

It is intended for those who may have gone through a certain amount of elementary music theory, say the fundamentals of traditional harmony as they are commonly taught, and may find themselves at odds with prevailing traits of that music which does not correspond to this knowledge. Presupposing such knowledge of the elements, the book does not stop to explain them, or to explain the terms which, if necessary, can be easily found in any music dictionary. It rather concentrates on material not incorporated in the current textbooks.

It is also intended for music lovers who desire to attain a better understanding—"appreciation"—of music at large; for practical musicians and amateurs who are aware of the incompleteness of their musical upbringing when confronted with a more progressive type of music; and finally for all those interested in trying their hand at musical composition. Thus it may well serve as a vade mecum for instruction or for self-instruction.

In the course of time, musical theory has developed certain divisions of detached analysis and study, such as harmony, counterpoint and so on, and has treated them individually. The division of theory into these branches is admissible only if we never, from beginning to end, lose sight of the close inter-relationship of the disciplines and their constant reciprocal influence and inter-dependence.

There is another item, fundamental enough to be put down at the outset and to be always kept in mind:

Beware of pedantry! Art resists any pedantic approach just as nature does. Neither art nor nature knows an unqualified "It must" or "It must not".

In art, as in nature, forces are at work which hardly ever —probably never—manifest themselves in pure, unbroken appearance; although the knowledge of their pure, unbroken appearance is necessary to understand the better their concourse and conflict. And even if we think we have caught everything we are at any time apt to encounter a freak which catches us by baffling and perhaps refreshing surprise.

In art and nature alike our knowledge is based primarily on observation of existing phenomena. In art and nature alike first comes creation; then, second in sequence, comes theory trying to describe and to explain. However, this sequence does not preclude that theory, in putting together its observations and drawing conclusions, may also by way of speculation and development pave the way for new discoveries or anticipate future events.

In pursuit of the principle that theoretical knowledge rests on observation of the existing, the ideas laid down in this book are exemplified almost exclusively by quotations from the living music literature of the past and the present. They are not intended to invite the student to copy and imitate. They are intended to stimulate his imagination and to inspire his own searching, discerning and, eventually, creative faculties.

In presenting this book to the music student at large, I wish to acknowledge that its formation owes much to the keen interest and the searching inquiries of my students over the years. The ultimate impulse to put my ideas down in the present form came from the response I received to a lecture series "The Shaping Forces in Music", delivered at Harvard University in fall 1944.

In the actual preparation of the book for publication, I am indebted to Dr. Max Krone and Robert Trotter for their valuable suggestions, and most of all to Dr. Gerald Strang for his able assistance in the final revision of the manuscript.

CONTENTS

HARMONY

MELODY

Contents

COUNTERPOINT

FORM

HARMONY

«Πάντα ῥεῖ»
(Everything is in flux)

Heraclitus

CHAPTER I

HARMONY AND CHORD

"Harmony" is the technical term for the coincidence of three or more different pitches.

So is "Chord".

This seems to imply that the two terms are identical.

Yet they are not; though in certain instances they may well be used for each other.

The symbols of Ex. 1, for example,

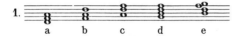

stand unequivocally for certain chords: *a* for triad, *b* and *c* for its two inversions (6-chord and $\frac{6}{4}$-chord respectively), *d* for 7-chord, *e* for its first inversion ($\frac{6}{5}$-chord). Yet they do not convey anything in the matter of *sound*, meaning *harmony*. They are like empty honeycombs, waiting to be filled with substance; dead skeletons in need of being awakened to life.

Any of the symbols of Ex. 2, put before them, will perform this transmutation.

Only now the symbols of Ex. 1 become unequivocally indicative of their sounds; only now the chords become *harmonies*. And though remaining the same chords — triad, 6-chord, 7-chord, etc. — they become different harmonies according to the application of the several clues of Ex. 2, a-d.

Bars 1 and 2 of Ex. 3 show a series of equal chords (6-chords) with constantly changing harmonies:

whereas Ex. 3a shows, with a single exception marked +, one unchanged harmony (the harmony of the *c* major tonic triad) in a series of changing chords:

We begin to sense that harmony is the far superior, far more relevant notion. It certainly is easier for the ear to distinguish two different harmonies than two different chord structures. It becomes evident that harmony has a greater bearing upon composition at large than chord; that harmony—not chord—may constitute part of the personal characteristics of different composers (Wagner, Debussy); that harmony, even within the same composition, has greater functional significance than chord. And it is finally safe to say that the functional significance of the chord recedes in the same measure as composition withdraws from the key-bound, tone-center-bound, degree-bound idiom of classical music, until, in completely a-tonal music, the chord-function practically vanishes to zero as compared with the harmony-function.

Still, while the functional value of the chord, even in classical music, is so much inferior to that of the harmony, it is present all the same.

To give a simple example: In the following cadential clause (Ex. 4a):

so familiar to us from countless occurrences that it hardly pays to select a special quotation, the two figured chords obviously reveal their harmonic identity. Yet they could not exchange their places (as shown in Ex. 4b) because of the definite *functional* (in this case cadential) mission of either chord.

Suppose we were to harmonize a simple phrase like the one of Ex. 5 in a simple way.

The folk tune offers, as most folk tunes do, for its most natural harmonization the use of the three basic harmonies I (tonic), V (dominant) and IV (sub-dominant):

Yet, planted there bluntly in their root positions (Ex. 6), the effect of these harmonies, correct as they are in themselves, would be rude as compared with Ex. 7.

Here the harmonies are the same, yet they partly exhibit an inverted chordal structure (6-chords in bars 2 and 3). In Ex. 6 the harmonies answer solely the several subsections opposite which they appear and to which they give the inherent harmonic support; yet they are wholly unconcerned with one another. They rigidly face their allotted melody portions and nothing else; among themselves they are poor neighbors. (The objectionable "consecutive fifths" are irrelevant under the present consideration.)

With the use of the chord-inversions (Ex. 7) this rudeness disappears instantly. The poor neighbors become good neighbors; that is, though still conscious of their primary task, at the same time they obligingly extend their hands, as it were, to their neighbors. *Harmonic* and *chordal* functions meet.

Theory usually attacks this problem by advising that each member of a harmony should take, on principle, the smallest step into membership in the neighboring harmony. While this axiom seems a simple and practical expedient for the beginner, it implants in him a dangerous misconception, namely the viewpoint of the rigidly *preconceived* harmony as a fixed unit, or pattern, within the frame of which each voice seeks to take up its appropriate place.

This narrow view must from the very beginning be replaced by the wider and superior view of the inherent urge of each voice toward linear self-preservation.

It is not enough to know that in the course of musical progression each tone asserts its membership in the harmony in which it is imbedded as well as in the melodic line of which it is part. The truth is that the melodic impulse is primary, and always preponderates over the harmonic; that the melodic, or linear, impulse is the force out of which germinates not only harmony but also counterpoint and form. For the linear impulse is activated by *motion,* and motion means life, creation, propagation and formation.

Just as the moving mists and clouds adopt the most diverse shapes in constant integration, diffusion and re-formation, thus the moving voices in music result in constantly changing harmonies.

To illustrate this point let us harmonize a short phrase like Ex. 8.

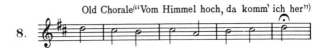

Old Chorale("Vom Himmel hoch, da komm' ich her")

Ex. 9 shows a most common, so to speak academic garden variety of such a harmonization:

There is really nothing wrong with this harmonization. Considering that it has to do with a chorale to be sung by or for a congregation in the church whose devotion it is meant to serve without deflecting their minds into conscious art-con- siderations, we may perfectly agree to it. However, taking this chorale melody, or just part of it, as a foil for demonstra- tion and study, we will forget about congregation and church and concentrate on our objective of showing how harmony may generate from linear impulses.

Ex. 10-21 show a variety of other harmonizations.

We suggest that the reader play singly first each of the four voices of each example. Next he might play any single voice together with the cantus firmus (the soprano). Only then should he play all four voices together, slowly, abiding for a while on each harmony in order to sense the desire, leaning and tendency of each harmony. Not too many variants should be tried at a time, so that the impressions may have a chance to settle.

Most of the harmonies as presented in Ex 10-21, if singled out and detached from their context, would prove nondescript in the light of traditional harmony. Everything opposed to it seems to be piled up: consecutive fifths, cross relations, spiteful coincidence of natural and altered steps, occasionally arbitrary dissonances. And yet we hope that the reader, even though these harmonizations may appear unusual and strange to him, will feel their logic and organic life. That they are arrived at by linear voice-leading, is obvious.

The principle of linear writing advocates melodic independence, which involves *movement* of voices. The principle of traditional harmonic writing, by assigning each voice its predetermined place, above all by making it sustain common tones of neighboring harmonies, suppresses melodic independence. It actually enslaves the voices, especially the middle voices, into the unconditional service of the task-master, harmony; whereas recognition of their inborn urge to move makes for a healthy democracy among all voices in which harmony thrives as well as melody.

A comparison of each single voice of Ex. 9 with each single voice of Ex. 10-21 will reveal this status. And their ensemble will reveal that the liberation of the voices triumphs over the fixed conception of harmony with all its implications, including its most dreaded shadow, the "dissonance".

Consonance and dissonance

In order to discuss these terms, we must first put aside their popular connotations of "beautiful" and "ugly". The identification of the "dissonance" with "cacophony" or, for that matter, with any aesthetic consideration whatsoever does not touch the technical significance of the term. Nor does the wholesale rejection of contemporary music of any epoch because of its "dissonances" differ in any way from the wholesale rejection of any innovation in any field of art or science before its general acceptance.

It would be hard indeed for us today to imagine that passages like Ex. 22 or 23 should have sounded "ugly" at any time:

So let us disregard any aesthetic considerations and approach the question from a purely technical viewpoint.

Dissonance can exist only if and where there exists consonance. The two terms are interconditioned as are big and small, light and dark, warm and cold. All these antagonistic concepts which suggest diametrical contrasts, are quite useful indeed as handy communication symbols of our everyday language. In reality, however, the terms of each pair are only different gradations of the same quality, or idea, or phenomenon. Physics does not know warmness and coldness, but just "heat", which covers the whole range from the lowest measurable or conceivable temperature ("degree of heat") to the highest. A certain definite temperature, felt as a chill if suddenly occurring in the tropics, will be felt as real heat in the arctic regions. Man is a huge giant as against the microbe, yet himself a microbe in the face of a glacier.

Between these two arbitrarily selected sizes are innumerable others, filing progressively by in an endless row. In the light of light there are countless shades of shade. At what point does the dark, the small, the cold cease and the light, the big, the warm begin?

No one will deny that the last chords of Ex. 22 and 23 are felt, after the preceding trembling tensions, as soothing and reconciling sounds endowed with all the intrinsic essence of the "consonance". And yet, in the practical everyday language of music these dominant seventh-chords are the prototypes of the dissonance, expected by theory to "resolve" into their respective triads—the prototypes of consonance.

For this is what theory declares: (1) That dissonance does not find repose in itself, and therefore does not satisfy the ear, but needs to "resolve", meaning to be followed by consonance, in which the ear may find repose and satisfaction; and (2) That certain sounds, intervals or harmonies are by nature dissonant, and others are by nature consonant. For instance seventh-chords are dissonant — a kind of black sheep; whereas triads are consonant — white sheep.

According to these fundamentals there can be no doubt left as to which of the two chords, seventh chord and triad, finds repose in itself and which does not; and therefore, which must resolve into which.

The following example (24) exposes a triad at + and a seventh-chord at ⊙.

If we stop playing at +, the want of repose, the urge to "resolve", in short, the dissonance-character of the chord as laid down by theory, is patent. Just as patent is the achieved repose, the hallmark of consonance, in the subsequent seventh chord at ☉. In fact, so strong is the urge of the dissonant *triad* at + to resolve that it impatiently anticipates by one eighth-note the craved-for resolution — into the *seventh chord*. Black and white sheep have quite naturally and peaceably exchanged their colors.

Here are a few classical quotations:

Disregarding chordal inversions, in Ex. 25 triad resolves into seventh-chord; in Ex. 26-31 dissonant triads resolve into consonant triads; in Ex. 25, 30, 31 the third is dissonant, in Ex. 26, 27 the fifth, in Ex. 28, 29 the root; in Ex. 26, 27 the dissonances form suspensions, in Ex. 25, 30, 31 passing tones, in Ex. 28, 29, appoggiaturas. Ex. 30, 31 exhibit quite capricious variants in that each juxtaposes one major and one minor triad, either being alternatively the resolution of the other.

So far it may be concluded beyond any discussion that no sound, considered by itself and detached from any context, can under any circumstances be other than neutral and meaningless, just as no letter of the alphabet can be anything but neutral and meaningless. To divide any kind of sounds, be it tones, intervals or harmonies, into one category of consonances *per se* — white sheep — and another one of dissonances *per se* — black sheep — is as absurd as it would be to divide the letters of the alphabet into consonances and dissonances.

The sooner we discard these two coddled pets of theory, the sooner we will discard with them an unending source of confusion. The future will look back at this doctrine of consonances and dissonances with the same pitying smile which we bestow upon the once-upon-a-time belief in witches and evil demons living inside certain individuals.

In the question of consonance and dissonance physics is not quite innocent in that it puts up the following, generally accepted statement: The simpler the ratio of the vibration-numbers of two tones, the more pleasant or "consonant" is their impression on the ear; the more complicated this ratio, the more unpleasant or "dissonant" is their impression.

This statement contains the following implications:

1. It identifies the terms consonant and pleasant, or dissonant and unpleasant.

2. It attributes the terms to definite, predetermined sounds (intervals in that case), independent of the context in which they appear.

It is not so surprising after all that the physicist or the physicists reponsible for this statement so far adopted the current maxims of the musical experts, since a scientist in one field would not hesitate to use for his own purposes the findings of the accredited authorities in another field. But the physical statement involves two more implications on which physics evidently departs from the theory of music and stands on its own feet, in fact points at qualities which musical theory so far has failed to acknowledge:

3. The statement of physics, in contrast to musical theory does *not* lay down any *absolute concept* of consonance and dissonance, thus suggesting the questionability of their existence as absolute phenomena.

4. It clearly suggests that they too, like warm and cold, etc., may be but different gradations of one quality, idea, or phenomenon.

While we heartily accept and acclaim the second pair of these implications, it requires little effort to refute the first pair.

According to the vibration ratio of the whole diatonic major scale, which is

$$1 : \frac{9}{8} : \frac{5}{4} : \frac{4}{3} : \frac{3}{2} : \frac{5}{3} : \frac{15}{8} : 2$$
$$_{c} \quad _{d} \quad _{e} \quad _{f} \quad _{g} \quad _{a} \quad _{b} \quad _{c^1}$$

the numeral relationship of the octave is the simplest of all, namely 1:2, while the vibration ratio of all the other intervals is represented by fractions. Thus, if among the intervals there should exist any "white sheep" at all, the octave must be the "whitest" of all. Contrasted to the ninth, whose vibration ratio, according to the continued table, would be $1 \cdot \frac{9}{4}$, there can again be no doubt as to which of the two is the consonance, which the dissonance and which the resolution of which.

We need but to reduce Ex. 24 to its outer contours (**Ex. 32**)

to see that this relationship of octave and ninth is flatly reversed. For it is evident that the octave in this case (+) does not find repose in itself, and therefore does not satisfy the ear, but needs to resolve into the subsequent ninth (⊙).

Thus it is with intervals as it is with chords: The urge to move onward in one case, and the satisfaction of this urge in another case, is as little inherent in certain predetermined intervals as it is in predetermined chords. These qualities are essentials of the moving voices that meet in intervals or chords.

If we play the voices of Ex. 32 *singly*, the urge to move on manifests itself in either voice as soon as it arrives at the point marked by +. The fact that the voices, at this point, meet in the interval of the octave, is purely accidental and without any consequence. *Any interval at this intersection would be bound to be dissonant.* Likewise any interval accidentally forming in the consistent course of two voices at the point of ⊚ would provide the resolution, as can be seen best by playing any combination of two voices of Ex. 24.

For in the end any sound—tone, interval or chord—once exposed to the force of attraction which emanates from the tonic, seeks to reach the tonic (dissolve, "resolve" into it) either directly or indirectly through the *sphere* of attraction that surrounds the tonic as its center.

Through this magnetic sphere, which is composed of all the secondary steps of the key (augmented sometimes by artfully altered, substituted, borrowed steps) the sound would gradually drift before finally yielding to the tonic. (See Ex. 78).

In order to activate this force of attraction, its center, the tonic—in other words the key—has first to be indubitably established. The reason why certain sounds in Ex. 24-32 show dissonance tendencies, in spite of their being consonances in the traditional sense, is that they are sharply exposed to their respective spheres of attraction. The reason why the harmonies of Ex. 39, 40 lack these dissonance tendencies, in spite of their being dissonances in the traditional sense, is that no tonic, that is, no center and no sphere of attraction, is given a chance to establish itself. Again, with the intentional suspension of any such tone center or center of attraction — the style that in our days is called "atonality" — the consonance-dissonance theory in any sense whatsoever is bound to collapse, and any attempt to apply its dogma must meet with perplexity and frustration.

Now this so-called atonality is a last stage of gradual evolution, a last conclusion drawn from ever present, if not always equally apparent principles.

The following example:

(*Andante*)   Chopin, Nocturne Op. 9 No. 2

33.

shows in bar 2, second half, a series of chords which progressively lead back to the key of E flat major. The charm of this progression lies in the fact that for a short stretch the power of attraction of the key-note *eb* is somehow suspended, or dimmed, and gradually reinstituted. We may say that this force is temporarily superseded by a stronger force—motion, momentum, inertia, whatever we may call it—until it asserts itself again and in turn supersedes the intermediate other force. Similarly, the vertically operating force of gravity may sometimes be neutralized by a stronger force effective in horizontal direction. Now if gravity can be neutralized at all, it makes no difference whether a moth flies through a room or an airship flies around the globe. Thus if the attracting force of the tonic can be neutralized at all, it makes no difference whether it is neutralized for no matter how short a passage of a musical piece or for a whole piece — atonality.

To come back now to Ex. 33: Let us for the sake of an illustrating experiment replace the progressions of bar 2 by other progressions as shown for instance in Ex. 34 and 34a.

The changes applied to the original are essential only in one point: while Chopin kept the composition within the traditional limits of chords of the third-system, the two variants present some tone-combinations that would defy such classification.

Ideologically, however, there is no difference between the original and the two variants. The musical function of the passage, namely the temporary suspension of the key and its reinstatement after the short episode, is certainly equally patent in all three versions. The preservation of the purity of style which would make such a replacement inconsistent with the rest of the composition must not blind us to the essential validity of the argument in question.

It would be out of place to view these substituted tone-combinations as "chords"; it would be equally out of place to view the original Chopin passage as "modulations" through different keys — with none of such keys established and none of the chords *in office,* though shamming the gown; but most of all, it would be out of place to view the original as containing one consonant chord—the *e* major triad—among dissonant chords, and the two variants as containing only dissonant chords.

The whole consonance-dissonance problem collapses again, its argument being beside the point.

The phases of the passage are not felt and cannot be interpreted as *either consonant or dissonant* but only as co-incidences of voices in motion, each of them propelled horizontally and creating its own momentum, and with it the momentum of the tone-combinations in which they happen to meet.

Thus they expose the real, intrinsic conception of harmony. For although harmony may still be defined as the combination of three or more tones, it has to be interpreted beyond this concept as a momentary situation brought about by moving voices; as the cross-section arising at times of arrested motion; or briefly and plainly as *arrested motion*.

It is the specific, momentary situation in midcourse of motion which endows a harmony with more or less momentum as the case may be; it is the absence of such motion which renders a harmony *per se* neutral.

A moving picture, stopped at a particular moment, may exhibit a group of people violently gesticulating, their faces passionately distorted. A newspaper picture may show a swimmer hovering in mid-air in perfect diving form, the diving board still vibrating from his take-off. A monument may show a rider on horseback, the horse rearing on its hind legs, the rider leaning forward, tightening the reins. We pass the movie scene, used perhaps for advertisement on a poster, time and again, without marveling that the people have not yet calmed down; the newspaper, lying around for any length of time, occasionally catches our eye and we do not marvel that the diver is still suspended in mid-air, the board still vibrating; the equestrian statue may outlive generations without anybody wondering at the strain of the pose. This is because our imagination automatically and empirically furnishes the missing real motion, of which, arrested at particular moments, these exposures are but visible symbols.

For *motion* it is, real or imaginary, that gives sense and meaning to these symbols, as it gives sense and meaning to the audible symbols. The very sentence I am writing now would leave me wondering and unsatisfied if stopped after any of its words except the last. Shall we now solemnly proclaim the word "LAST", — l-a-s-t — a consonance and the rest of those words dissonances, demon-possessed witches? Any word may be the first, the middle or the last of a sentence. And so the mediaeval witch-burners were doubly wrong; first because no girl is a witch and second because all girls are witches.

And as to harmonies — they all are consonances and they all are dissonances; or rather, harmony, consonance and dissonance, they all are the same — the same substance, or phenomenon, or idea — *arrested motion.*

CHAPTER II

HARMONY AS ARRESTED MOTION

In the light of the foregoing considerations, the difference between the notions "harmony" and "chord" clears up and broadens.

While the notion "chord" carries much more the flavor of something solid, static, substantial, measurable; the "harmony" notion implies the aspect of the fluid, unsubstantial, immeasurable. We may say chord is to harmony as body is to soul; or harmony is the soul of the chord. It may suit the chord, the honeycomb frame of combined intervals, to enter classification by measurements and mathematical symbols. If we try to force harmony into such rigid objectivity, it escapes this compulsion by a hundred loopholes.

Even our everyday language senses this difference of meaning — the technical narrowness of the chord-notion as against the trans-technical implications of the harmony-notion. We speak of spheric harmonies but not of spheric chords; and Pythagoras and his followers, innocent of future harmony textbooks with figured bass and the like, were uninhibited in visualizing, or "audializing", these *harmonies* of the spheres. Similarly we speak of eternal harmony, a harmonious person, a harmonious marriage, but not of an eternal chord, a chordal person, a chordal marriage. Behind the corporeal substantiality of the chord hides the sensitive soul of harmony.

It is worthwhile to know about the chords, their structure and consistency and it is commendable for the beginner to learn about them as a kind of foundation and a serviceable basis of communication. But if he stops at this system he will be at the mercy of fatal limitations, inhibitions and perplexities; he will be doomed *not to see the forest for the trees.*

Beware of restraining the harmony phenomenon in a prison of mathematical symbols. It will revolt against such constraint and it will baffle you. If you want to penetrate to its core and disarm it, you must leave your measurements and figures at home and approach it, as it were, unarmed yourself. Heraclitus' basic principle «Πάντα ῥεῖ» ("everything is in flux") will serve you better as a sesame to open the door and win to the heart of harmony.

It is from such a vantage point that the infinite expressiveness of the definite "harmony", even in the classical vocabulary, becomes luminous. What seems to recur again and again in the same outer appearance, is in fact a different substance in each different concatenation of events.

The influence of the situation

Do you know about the hydraulic cycle? It is so perfectly closed in itself that no one can tell where it starts. Chemistry calls water H_2O. But this H_2O is given in a continuous chain of situations, each a link between others. The cloud, the rain-drop, drizzle and cloud-burst; the snow-flake and the single snow-crystal, sleet, the hail-stone, and ice; fog and dew; the spring, the brook, the stream, the ocean; vapor and steam — which is the real H_2O? It is liquid, solid and gaseous; it is without color, light-green and dark-blue. Even the rainbow is H_2O under certain conditions, in a certain situation. Put the tone in place of the molecule and you have the multiplicity of its appearances. Put the harmony in place of the drop and you get the multiplicity of its situations. What else is $\frac{5}{3}$ here than H_2O there? Both symbols are serviceable tools for a certain approach. But the one should not be more to the musician than the other is to the painter or the poet. He must be able to entirely forget about them when he approaches the work of art, be it as creator, percipient, or student of harmony.

A few illustrations will show harmony in different situations. In Ex. 35

the function, or the "situation", of the two fundamental harmonies of the key (tonic and dominant) is such that they simply and obviously give support to the equally simple melody. The composition is so essentially and exclusively rooted in the melody that it would clearly and unmistakably convey its meaning even without the actual sounding of the (by nature quasi) inherent harmonization.

In Ex. 36

the situation is exactly reversed. Here nothing exists to be harmonized at all. The composition rests entirely in the progression of harmonies, as many other works of Bach do. So utterly unessential to the composer seem all events which could possibly be grouped around those harmonies that he leaves them completely to the discretion of the improvising player. To be sure, the art of improvisation in those times was highly developed but it is difficult to say what was the cause and what the effect. In other cases of similar order Bach himself would add such an improvisation, as for instance in the first Prelude of the "Well-tempered Clavichord". The special pattern of broken chords established by the composer is so familiar to us that we would consider it a crime to change it. But to Bach's contemporaries it would have appeared perfectly natural to vary the given pattern of chord-breaking (Ex. 37) by other patterns such as Ex. 37a and 37b, as they were accustomed to do in so many other compositions of this type where it was actually left to them.

In the following example

the situation of harmony is about midway between its situations in the two preceding quotations by Schubert and Bach. Here the musical event is based neither on the bare melody nor on the bare harmony. Equivalent in measure and weight, the one dissolves in the other like a tablet in water, into a homogeneous substance. As support here, almost more for rhythmical accentuation than actual harmonization, the sparse touches of the bass are sufficient.

In Ex. 39 and 40

chords line up which all show the same interval-structure. The fact that this structure makes each of them a dominant-ninth of some major key seems to be of little import. None of them accepts the consequence of its ninth, of its position on the dominant, or of its membership in any key. Both passages exhibit a chain of ninth-chords none of which even so much as attempts to "resolve" in any way. With the temporary suspension of any established key (just by the very chain of isolated new dominants) the feeling of the dissonance-quality, that is, the urge for resolution of these chords, disappears. They have ceased to possess a causal relation of tonality to each other or to a common tone-center. The relation of tonal causality gives way to the mere sensation of a "sound-impression" *per se*.

Again harmony has entered a new situation. That it still retains — an item of utter unimportance — the outer garment of a chord of the third-system may be attributed to a last residue of conscience in which the composer was steeped by tradition and education. If the chord-pattern were even more dissonant in the traditional sense its effect could (and most probably would) be still softer, still more iridescent, still more "impressionistic". At any rate, in spite of third-structure and compatibility with the old classification, harmony has abandoned entirely its static, objective quality.

In Moussorgsky's "Boris Godunow" (Ex. 41) a long
scene — people praying in front of a church — is illustrated
musically by two constantly alternating harmonies:

Moussorgsky, "Boris Godunow"

41.

To the harmonies are added (apart from changes in orchestration) various patterns of chord-breaking in the high registers of the orchestra such as:

42.   43.

But aside from this—with reference to themes, melodic development, musical flow, etc.—nothing happens. Here also
the two harmonies are dissonant chords of the third-system,
the most simple and the most frequent: dominant seventh
chords expected by tradition to resolve into the tonic some
time. But who now recognizes them as such, who now
would think with the first one of *db* major or minor and

with the second one of *g* major or minor, the only keys to which they belong? They never resolve and no one misses a resolution. They support no melody and no one misses a melody. They establish no key and no one misses a key.

Detached from any harmonic or melodic causality, liberated from the ties of their origin, they are but sounds freely floating around in space, harmony in its aboriginal power and without any other musical consequence, like the sound of church-bells, mighty and primordial in their effect as we may imagine the "harmony of the spheres". Again the outer garment of their chordal structure and their apparent membership in certain keys is purely accidental. Again it was a last inhibition which, for all the lure and for all the power of his vision, restrained the composer from shaking off the fetters of third-bound theory.

He who in the sparkling tone-glitter of the silver-rose in Strauss' "Rosenkavalier" (Ex. 44, 44a)

R. Strauss, "Rosenkavalier"

should attempt to refer the sounds to the common denominator of the "figured bass" would soon have to desist. Still, it can hardly be imagined that the lovely and so "false" celeste-chords should ever have hurt anyone's ear. Do they not in their light-refractions and tone-reflections come strikingly near to the "rainbow" situation of the substance H_2O?

Yet with all these manifestations of an impressionistic sound-expression the non-static, fluid character of the harmony-phenomenon is not exhausted. They only represent another outlet among the many through which at different times, with more or less timidity or determination, harmony made its way into the open. Besides, the examples from "Rosenkavalier" need not be evaluated only from the viewpoint of impressionism. They emanate also from another point, the coincidence of different *"streams"*. It would obviously be absurd to relate what goes on in the moving chords of the upper register to the harmonies sustained in the lower register. The latter form a sound-community united by one idea, or one harmonic will; the chord-group fleetingly drifting above it another community, united by another idea, or harmonic will. In this case it happens that the group of sustained harmonies adheres to one tone-center, or key; the group in motion, unattached to any such center, revolves loosely around the first.

The simultaneity of such sound-streams is one of the chief reasons for the repudiation of the conception of harmony as a static object rooted in structural patterns.

At the bottom of a musical phrase like Ex. 45

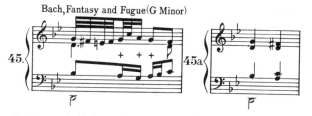

Bach, Fantasy and Fugue (G Minor)

lies the interminably recurring cadential formula of Ex. 45a. But the voices of the soprano and tenor, moving linearly,

clash in the triple coincidence of the tones *g* and *a,* marked
+, while they struggle to free themselves from the firm grip
of the cadential harmonies. (Note also the *c* in the soprano.)

Only from the viewpoint of linear streams can such
sounds as the ones marked in Ex. 46 be judged at all.

Beethoven, Sonata Op. 53

But such sounds in their tame and playfully ornamental
form are hardly noticeable nor are they characteristic of
Beethoven's sometimes provocative recklessness. In Ex. 47
the linear voice-leading takes on a considerably different
appearance.

Beethoven, Sonata Op. 90

The shortness of the phrase does not render its conception less linear. Moreover it is written for such a percussive
sound quality as the piano and lies most awkwardly for the
player. This is one of the many instances to show how little
Beethoven cared about an easy technical sleekness and how
exclusively he was concerned with the pursuit of the abstract
idea — in this case the imitation of the motif in stretto.

Likewise unconcernedly he interpenetrates tonic triad and dominant seventh-chord in the following stretto:

Beethoven, Sonata Op.81a

The boldness of this example consists in the concurrence of those four tones embracing the most heterogeneous harmonies, tonic and dominant, so to speak the positive and negative poles. Thus the complete mutual penetration of these polar harmonies flashes up momentarily. The following little phrase contains the same tone-structures (Ex. 49, +):

Where did the boldness vanish all of a sudden? The phrase is not a quotation from an existing classical composition, yet invented so much in the classical idiom that it easily could occur in any such composition. Belonging no longer to two different streams — the polar harmonies of tonic and dominant — the sound-compounds have changed their *situations* completely.

In another passage, famous and much disputed for that reason, Beethoven puts the two polar harmonies directly and unexpectedly into one another:

Theory with its *idée fixe* of the systematized chordal structures, regarding harmony as a solid object, finds itself-puzzled and cornered by such unruliness. Anxious, nevertheless, to keep up its dogma, it resorts to excuses and subterfuges, administers "exceptional" privileges, issues special passports and remains stubbornly blind to the fact that the crisis, scantily patched up at one point, is bound to recrudesce unexpectedly at a hundred other points. What is the good of finding terms for all the emerging "non-harmonic" events? Will it really help in the end? Will it strike home? If we acquiesce at the "free anticipation" of Ex. 50, what about Ex. 48, let alone 44 and 44a? Shall we call the *f* in the tenor of Ex. 48, bar 3, a "passing tone"? In point of fact this example alone, written one and a half centuries ago, should suffice to elucidate the whole issue. Moreover, it should suffice to point out, from one viewpoint at least, the constant, inevitable, illimitable evolution of harmony to come.

Solid objects are subject to the law of impermeability; but not sounds. Not being solid objects, they can easily penetrate each other. In Ex. 48 two harmonic streams, we may say two sound beams, penetrate each other as two light beams would do; and the image of their intersections is the image

of their motion arrested at those particular moments. As two
or more light-beams would produce a certain color at the
point of their intersection, unforeseen perhaps, yet easily
intelligible as the result of its several color components;
similarly, two or more sound-beams produce a certain harmony at the point of their intersection, not preconceived,
classified or classifiable, yet intelligible for the ear as the
result of its sound components and in no need of any excuse,
exceptional privilege or passport.

If we play a scale of sixth-chords in contrary motion as
shown in Ex. 51,

the resulting harmonies are sufficiently explained by the two
moving streams and we need not bother about their particular appearances, their individual registration and classification. They are bound to produce an intelligible, logical
and *pleasant* impression.

Venturing one step further, we may as well combine
two such streams which no longer belong to the same key
(Ex. 52 and 52a):

or, in other variants (Ex. 53 and 53a) change the keys midcourse of each stream:

The logic still holds good; the sounds still penetrate each other readily and, if anything, affect us as being still more velvety than if they belonged to the same key. At the same time, they vouchsafe a glimpse into "polytonality" (Ex. 52, 52a) or expose coincidences of "borrowed", or "vicarious" tones (Ex. 53, 53a). These two latter features often overlap, their borderline being hard to define.

Of course, in actual composition independent streams need not and will not appear just in scales; nor need each stream express full harmonies, but they may partly or wholly be reduced to lines. In other words harmonies may combine with harmonies (Ex. 54, 56, 60, 63), or harmonies may combine with lines (Ex. 57, 59, 61), or lines may combine with lines (Ex. 62a).

Here are a few illustrations:

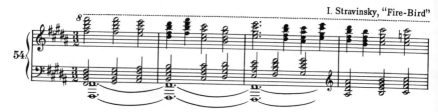

(monotonal)

(monotonal)

(polytonal)

(polytonal)

Shostakovich, Prelude Op. 34 No. 9

58.

(polytonal)

Roy Harris, Sonata Op. 7

59.

(polytonal)

ibidem

60.

(streams establishing no key)

Aaron Copland, "Sentimental Melody"

61.

(polytonal or vicarious steps)

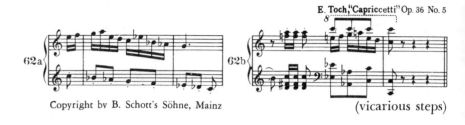

(vicarious steps)

(streams establishing no key)

By vicarious steps we understand altered — more frequently lowered than raised — steps. Their use abundantly prevails in classical music. Here are a few examples.

Ex. 64-66 show the low second step (supertonic) instead of its normal, or authentic form. In Ex. 67-70 the respective authentic and vicarious pitches are playfully juxtaposed:

Still, the actual coincidence, the complete interpenetration of such authentic steps and their vicarious forms, is somehow alien to the classical idiom.

Ex. 71-73 show authentic and vicarious pitches in stringent interpenetration:

One needs but to restore equality of the unruly pitches by playing either *f* or *f♯* in Ex. 71, and either *d* or *d♯* in Ex. 72, in both melody and harmony (in short in both hands) to feel the dullness of such attempted "rectification", as against the succulence of the original. The two passages reveal the sure and uninhibited instinct of the composer.

Harmonies are not solid objects.

As has been said, Ex. 48 would suffice to confirm this axiom and point out the direction of the evolution of harmony at least from one angle, the interpenetration of harmonic streams.

CHAPTER III

THE EXPANDING HARMONIC UNIVERSE

In the preceding discussion of interpenetrating harmonic streams, each stream derived its interval structure from the traditional method of superposing thirds (including even passages of such contemporary diction as Ex. 59-63). If we consider, however, that the method of superposing thirds is not the only generating source of harmonies, the harmonic scope widens considerably.

Perfect fourths or fifths, superposed on one another, travel through all our twelve half-tones before returning to the starting point. Thus they form a completely closed circle, which gives them the advantage over the thirds of incomparably greater variety for harmonic building material. As to tonality, a series of seven perfect fourths or fifths still belong to one major key, embracing all its seven steps.

Ex. 74a, b show such fourth-harmonies in monotonality (a) and polytonality (b).

If we further consider that these intervals can also be altered (augmented fourth, diminished fifth) and harmonies may contain both perfect and altered forms of fourths or fifths, the harmonic scope again widens considerably.

Ex. 75 shows a motif employing such harmonies.

Besides, we must also remember that our diatonic major and minor scales are not the only possible ones to be taken as bases for composition. Many other scales, containing seven steps or more or less, have been constructed and used by some composers, e.g. Slonimsky, Tscherepnine, and Holst. Nor need the row of our twelve half-steps be confined to the space of one octave, but may be parcelled out within a two-octave space, omitting the first perfect octave or any other repetition of pitch. It is evident that by such practice again the harmonic scope is bound to widen. There is also, of course, the whole-tone scale.

True, should all these leads be followed up exhaustively, one would arrive at intersecting results occasionally and certain sound-combinations would appear as simultaneously belonging to different systems. Even so, measured against the vast array of harmonic combinations that these considerations are bound to afford, must not the few miserable chords tabulated by traditional theory appear as a pitifully poor stock?

How proudly do we display certain findings like the "Neapolitan sixth" or the "augmented sixth"! Is not one passage like Ex. 64 enough to reveal the former's true nature, sixth or no sixth? Does it not evidence the full citizenship of the low supertonic in the key — root-position or inversion? And do not the subsequent examples up to Ex. 73 exhibit the whole argument — the *exchangeability of low and high steps* — in a nutshell? We certainly would not interpret bars 2 and 6 of Ex. 69 as composed in the key of *c* minor, in the midst of a lengthy *c* major passage. Nor did the composer of Ex. 70 mean to change the *key* in bars 2 and 4.

The activating cause of these two passages is rather to be found in their *melodies* which employ both the low and high forms of one step alternately and thus occasion an incidental change of harmony.

It happens at times that some authentic member of the key, altered into its substitute, appears *by chance* imbedded in a harmony which is still simple and familiar to us by old acquaintance, a specimen of the third system. The altered step in such a case remains inconspicuous and we accept the substituted harmony without further ado; in fact its disguise makes us apt to misinterpret its true nature by taking for a harmonic event what in reality is a sheer melodic event. Such is the case in Ex. 69, 70 (cf. also Ex. 30, 31).

At other times, however, it happens that such an alteration produces a harmony which, *by chance again,* no longer coincides in appearance with a familiar one but makes the altered step somehow protrude conspicuously beyond the familiar chordal frame. Such is the case in Ex. 67.

The promoting idea in Ex. 67, 68 and 69 is always the same: the playful alternation of an authentic and its vicarious step as a *sheer melodic event.*

In Ex. 69 this altered step happens to be the third; in Ex. 67 and 68 the supertonic, the "Neapolitan" pitch. In Ex. 68 the playful turn of the melody lies in the upper voice, in Ex. 67 it happens to lie in the bass.

Inconspicuous harmonically in its authentic form, (Ex. 76, at +) , it instantly becomes harmonically conspicuous in

its altered form (⊚) . And instantly we pounce upon it, tag and needle drawn, and pin the label on it. A new harmony has been discovered, hallelujah! Triumphantly we parade it, put it in a shrine and worship it. The collection of chords has been increased by one. Now the student of harmony, if he wants to cover all of it, has to add to his knowledge of triads, seventh-chords, ninth-chords and their possible inversions not only the Neapolitan sixth, but also the *"augmented"* sixth. Does that not sound like a student of botany flaunting his complete knowledge of the vegetable kingdom by enumerating exhaustively the oak, the buttercup, the string bean, the daisy and the walnut?

We are surrounded by an ocean of plants. But we are indeed surrounded by an ocean of harmonies as well. Why do we shut our eyes to this fact? Is it because we shrink from the Gargantuan task of labelling them all, and from the super-Gargantuan task of committing them to memory? There is an easy way out: Stop attempting to label them by measures and symbols. Stop regimenting them as though they were solid objects. Give up the stubborn, unfruitful view of the static and adopt the more productive view of the instantaneous image of an ever-fluid, ever-fluctuating, ever-gyrating phenomenon; the view of the ever-changing relation of a stellar body to the rest of the universe, the view of the Heraclitean axiom, "Everything is in flux."

Subdivision of the half-tone

All these investigations were based on our system of twelve half-tones, the product of the subdivision of the perfect octave into twelve tolerably equal tone-spaces. This subdivision is by no means an irrefragable, God-given or nature-given fact. Rather we know it to be agreed upon by convention based on artistic — musical — as well as scientific — physical — considerations. Who tells us that this subdivision is the only feasible one? In fact we know that between these half-tones lie an infinite number of other pitches. Moreover, this fact is known to us not only theoretically, but by real and frequent physical experience, strange as it may seem, and in spite of our being unheedful of it.

How particular is a conductor about his orchestra being in perfect tune before starting to play! And how particular is he about having his men play all the pitches as pure and clean as possible! (And justly so!) Yet he does not mind in the least — nor does the audience — hearing the purest harmony blurred, muddled up, in fact all but wiped out, by the collateral roll of a snare drum, the crash of a cymbal, the beat of the bass drum, the gong or the tamtam, the peal of chimes or the mere tinkling of the triangle. Where does his — and our — harmonic conscience vanish all of a sudden?

True, we accept these sounds as incidental and somehow detached from the harmonic events. Yet we cannot deny that their complex sounds contain, beside their material characteristics, numerous nondescript interjacent pitches which could be sifted and bared by acoustical instruments.

A violinist may tune his instrument first to the pitch of one piano and next to the pitch of another piano, perhaps considerably different from the first. Along with the four strings, the whole tonal system, with all the overtones and all the slumbering harmonies, will change by a quarter-tone, more or less.

Suppose someone sings a passage of some length and intricacy, unaccompanied. At the end of it the pitch may show quite a perceptible drop, though the infinitesimal phases of gradual dropping may be hardly discernible. Nor will it actually hurt the ear; and if some musicians make a great fuss over the shortcoming, it will be rather for reasons of professional ostentation than of actual pain. Putting aside all prejudices of training and education, we must admit that the passage as sung by the culprit represents a modulation from one key into another. And if smoothness, evenness, gradualness and imperceptibility constitute professional virtues of such a transition, we must further admit that no school-modulation can rival this accidental one in these qualities.

What happened? The singer started in one key "X" and finished in another key "Y", say one half tone or so lower. He arrived at this somewhat remote key (remote in the sense of key-relationship) not by way of "legitimate" modulation but by smooth and gradual gliding throughout the passage, as indicated by the diagonal in the diagram (Ex. 77).

On his way he necessarily touched upon a number of other interjacent keys (indicated in the diagram by parallel horizontal lines) or at least used some of their inherent pitches. If he should try to produce this "modulation" intentionally, self-consciousness would probably prevent him from succeeding. The smoothness would be gone.

Does not the idea offer itself to utilize such accidents, to elevate them from the level of casualness to the level of planned organization?

The idea of splitting the half-tone space is old. Since the advent of this century a number of technicians as well as composers have engaged themselves in the production and utilization of sub-halftones (Stein, Möllendorf, Mager, Wishnegradsky, Theremin, Ives, Bartók and above all the Czech composer Alois Hába). During the International Music Festival at Frankfort on Main in 1927 I attended a lecture of Hába on the subject in which he sang for exemplification a chromatic row of quarter-tones and sixth-tones, testing every second quarter-tone or every third sixth-tone by the coinciding chromatic half-tone on the piano. Not only were the pitches distinctly discernible but the ear became used to them quickly, and their scales soon took on an effect equivalent to that of our familiar chromatic scale.

Though such experiments and speculations have no direct bearing on the elemental gift of creative genius, their preparatory value for future music is patent and undeniable. After all it was the tempered system of our twelve tones, arrived at by experiments as well, into which the composers of the past cast their ideas, lighting upon this system through the accidental date of their birth; as poets would use the language into which they were born by accident of date and place.

Speculative as such an approach to quarter-tone music appears, and cryptic as its sound is bound to remain as long as it is not heard and practised generally, it still is not mere technical experiments or academic reflections that point to the use of quarter-tones or otherwise subdivided half-tones. Again it is classical music itself which suggests harmonic evolution in this direction; which, in fact, actually raps at the very gates of sub-halftone music.

In Ex. 78 (somewhat simplified for easier reading or

Brahms, Clarinet-Quintet Op. 115

playing) the three chords which perform the modulation back to b major (⊢———⊣) obviously owe their origin to the linear movement of the three lower voices against the sustained upper voice. The plastic effect of these moving voices, pointed up by the composer through the added dynamics ($<$ $>$), manifests itself easily to the ear and can be perceived still better if the voices are played singly, one after the other.

The *c* in the cello at the downbeat of bar 7 has a double function. First it continues the preceding upbeat, still supporting the vicarious, Neapolitan-fashioned *c* major triad. But presently it assumes the import and function of a *b♯*, preparing for and leading into the subsequent *c♯*.

The double spelling of the pitch in Ex. 79a is intended to make this change of meaning more evident.

Were the meaning of *c♮* to prevail throughout the bar, its tendency either to stay in the key or to move downward as shown in Ex. 79b, would suggest itself; contrariwise the interpretation of an obtaining *b♯* would suggest its growing out of the lower step *b♮*, as shown in Ex. 79c.

The sensitive string player (or singer) will in such cases instinctively adjust the pitch to the tendencies of the particular context. He will take the same pitch higher for example if it represents the "leading-tone" than if it represents the seventh in a dominant seventh-chord, thus increasing the magnetic tension by increased approximation to the goal tone.

Consequently, if the cellist wants to do justice to the

changing meaning of the *c* in this passage, as shown in Ex. 79a, he would have to actualize this change by raising the pitch of the leading-tone-like *b*♯ above the pitch of the *c* — the fusion of these two pitches into one being but a compromise of the "tempered" system.

The final solution offers itself with compelling logic. It is shown in Ex. 79d, introducing the quarter-tone above the *c*, as indicated by the arrow pointing upwards. (The arrow pointing downwards is suggested for the quarter-tone below, as applied in Ex. 80b).

Needless to say, this experiment is not meant to "correct" the composition but to demonstrate the issue in question.

It may be objected, however, that the introduction of the eighth-notes in bar 7 somehow disturbs the rhythmical evenness of the modulatory passage. It seems indeed very likely that the composer's concern was to bring about the modulation by equally moving voices, adjusting the motion of the two lowest voices rhythmically to the motion of the second violin which obviously holds the lead in this passage. Starting from a *c* major triad, however, the two lowest voices had no way of moving by steps. The alternative for them would be either to be sustained over the bar-line and wait for their release after the downbeat (Ex. 80a) or to move

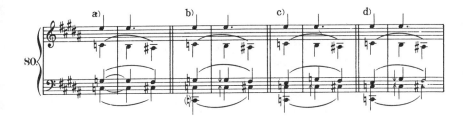

within their own harmonic organism. Preferring any kind
of motion to stagnation, the composer chose the latter way
(Ex. 78), thereby gaining at least the amenity of the "encircling approach" (see page 118) in the viola part.

Only the use of quarter-tones could have satisfied both
desirabilities—the preservation of the two harmonic corner-
pillars and their linking by even, stepwise convergence in
the several voices over the middle chord (Ex. 80b). Or the
encircling turn of the viola part could also be retained if so
desired (Ex. 80c or 80d).

Ex. 81 shows a similar condition.

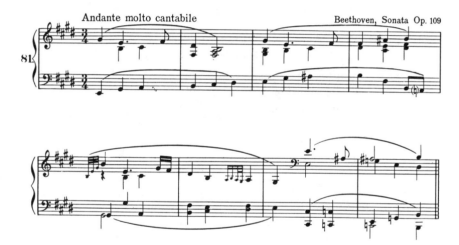

Throughout the whole phrase an even rhythm of quarter-notes is maintained in the accompaniment, carried chiefly
by the bass. Occasionally the melodic flow of this voice produces unpreconceived harmonies by its linear passage (middle of bars 2 and 6).

Around the advent of the last bar, however, this smooth

rhythmical flow of the bass is balked for three beats, there being no more moving space left for the descending voice. Similarly to Ex. 78 the middle voices take over the maintenance of the rhythm by shifting inside the harmonic organism. And similarly to Ex. 78 the problem could be solved by the use of quarter-tones as shown in Ex. 82a.

Also, the middle voices could be retained, sharing now the rhythmical responsibility and at the same time enriching the harmony (Ex. 82b).

It is recommended that this quarter-tone passage of the bass be sung, while playing the rest of the voices on the piano. One will be surprised at the facility of the task, its novelty being sufficiently eased by its tangible logic.

Whether or not the composers of Ex. 78 and 81 would have chosen to use quarter-tones, presuming their availability at those times, is of no interest. The point is that their practicability is sufficiently proved to make them eligible for use at whatever time.

We need not actually hear the quarter-tone harmonies of Ex. 80 and 82 in order to be sure of their musical logic. For we know they originate with the same logic as for instance the likewise linearly derived harmonies in Ex. 10-21 and therefore must be intelligible, logical and "beautiful".

Furthermore we have come to understand that no harmony *per se,* and therefore none of these quarter-tone harmonies *per se* either, can be anything but neutral and that here again it is their derivation and placement which renders them intelligible, logical and "beautiful".

At one time, it was just the augmented sixth which ventured forth timidly or boldly, as we may view it; and though propelled by a merely melodic impulse and innocent of any harmonic plot, it was pinned down as an isolated, solitary freak of harmony. Yet the hiding-place from which it escaped, this same melodic propulsion, proved and keeps proving an inexhaustible cornucopia of such freaks. The harmonies of Ex. 10-21 as well as the quarter-tone harmonies of Ex. 80 and 82 are nothing else. (Incidentally, the quarter-tone step in Ex. 82b makes the augmented sixth an augmented augmented sixth, which could be further augmented by simultaneously raising the $a\sharp$ to its higher quarter-tone.)

Naturally, the eventual introduction of quarter-tones means no displacement of the old chromatic twelve-tone scale but merely its amplification. In the same way and measure as the twelve tones permit the melodic and harmonic use of both diatonic and chromatic pitches, the twenty-four tones still leave at the discretion of the composer the choice, melodically or harmonically, of any diatonic, semi-tonal or quarter-tonal system and any arbitrary mixture of them. We may compose completely atonal music with the twelve half-tones and completely tonal music with twenty-four (or more) sub-halftones, as we have seen in Ex. 80 and 82.

Moreover, we must beware of linking any kind of existing art-material with any kind of personal style, approach or conception of the artist.

The juxtaposition of the two following excerpts (Ex. 83, 84) may throw some light on this subject.

83.

Slow, ♩ = 56

A. Schönberg "Pierrot Lunaire," Op. 21

84.

con molto passione

Ex. 83, though still confined to the twelve half-tones, is far the more radical of the two. It reveals the last consequences of linear writing, in its fine-pencilled fabric producing a harmonic-melodic web of prismatic tenuity.

Ex. 84 on the other hand, in spite of the drastic innovation of the quarter-tones, is, rather, suggestive of the classical style of quartet writing somewhere in the neighborhood of, say, Schumann, with the first violin holding the lead and the three lower voices subdued almost to the task of harmonization, though the tone-material of such harmonization be ever so amplified.

Common to both, however, is the fact that each defies any attempt at a harmonic analysis in the old sense and that both afford a glimpse into the vastness of harmonic variety.

Nor need we, speaking of this vastness, be vague about its numerical realities. In passing, it might well be worthwhile to take a more precise account of such harmonic possibilities.

If we take any four-pitched harmony such as one of our common and familiar seventh-chords, and subject the four pitches to alterations by half-tones or quarter-tones, the number of combinations without repetitions is 625 (namely m^n if n represents the number of the chord-members and m the number of their five appearances — original, raised by half-tone, raised by quarter-tone, lowered by half-tone, lowered by quarter-tone). Ex. 80b shows one of these 625 possible varieties of the original, with its root raised and its fifth lowered both by quarter-tones.

A six part fourth-harmony such as contained in Ex. 74a or b would yield 15625 varieties without repetition.

In the perfect-fourth harmony continued to its end (over five octaves) or the perfect-fifth harmony continued to its end (over seven octaves) we would have to renounce all the alterations by half-tones, for since these harmonies embrace in their anatomy all the 12 tones of our chromatic scale, any half-tone alteration of one of their members would mean 'the repetition of its chromatic neighbor. Thus *m* in this case is reduced from 5 to 3, (original, raised by quarter-tone, lowered by quarter-tone,) and the resulting number of combinations of such a chord is *only* 531441.

If we disregard quarter-tones entirely and confine ourselves to our system of twelve tempered half-tones, the composer still has at his disposal 4017 different harmonies from three to twelve tones, whereby only the actual pitches are counted regardless of their spelling, their arrangement by intervals or position, in short anything pertaining to chordal structure.

But with all this knowledge we must never lose sight of the more important fact that harmony itself, of three pitches or whatever number, of half-tone or whatever extended system, is but the casual, incidental image of arrested motion, of ever-fluctuating situation, ever-changing meaning and effect.

Looking at what has been achieved in the development of musical material so far, let us enjoy the thought that only a tiny portion of the soil has been tilled as yet, and that by far the major part of work and harvest still lies ahead of us, including that focus of eternal lure and fascination — harmony.

MELODY

Das höchste ist die Gunst, womit der Himmel schaltet,
Das nächste ist die Kunst, womit der Gärtner waltet.

Fr. Rückert, *"Die Weisheit des Brahmanen"*

CHAPTER IV

MELODY VERSUS HARMONY

Would an attempt to treat of melody in a technical way be a presumption? Melody — the very essence of "divine inspiration", bestowed upon chosen master-minds by the grace of God, the most intimate utterance of musical genius, prompted directly by "the voices of angels, the chant of the birds, the murmur of the purling brook or the spell of the silvery moonlight"?

Such conceptions seem to account for the strange fact that so much is being written, taught and studied about harmony and so little, if anything at all, about melody.*

Certainly melody is a matter of inspiration. But so, no less and no more, is harmony. Or are we to assume that Wagner's "Tristan and Isolde", this richest mine of harmonic beauty and novelty, was the fruit of the composer's particular industry in the study of harmony? Nor is counterpoint, nor is form, nor is any artistic skill in any artistic field detachable from inspiration. The one is nothing without the other; both have to meet and to work together.

---

* The author's first ideas on this subject were laid down in his "Beiträge zur Stilkunde der Melodie" (University of Heidelberg, 1921) and later on in his "Melodielehre" (Max Hesse's Verlag, Berlin 1923).

Nature, intuition, inspiration are one thing; analysis, study, skill are another thing. From time immemorial the human mind has tried to hitch both to the star of human progress.

The diamond, as presented by nature, would elicit little enchantment. It takes the highest skill of the cutter, practiced, cultivated and improved through many generations, to make it the coveted jewel. At the same time this accomplished art of the cutter would be a pitiful waste, utterly lost and ineffectual, without nature's gift of the raw diamond.

Every composer knows, and many sketches of the masters give ample proof, that there is a long and hard road from the first inspiration to its final form. And since this applies to melody in the same degree as to harmony and all the rest of the craft, it certainly must appear worthwhile to undertake an analysis of melody, to hearken to the possible forces at work in melody, as in the other musical phenomena, and to make the knowledge of them responsive to the technique of composition.

*   *   *

Melody, though closely interlinked with harmony, differs from it in two fundamental points.

1. While harmony is marked by the temporal *coincidence* of different pitches, melody is marked by their temporal *succession*.

2. While harmony, being a momentary situation, is completely detached from any rhythmical events, such rhythmical events represent a basic and most vital component of melody.

In a harmony the arrangement of the coinciding pitches (interval structure) is irrelevant. A change of their order does *not* change the harmony, as shown in Ex. 3; it has no bearing on the harmony. With the temporal *succession* of pitches, however — the mark of melody — their order becomes most essential. A change of this order changes the melody considerably, as revealed in Ex. 85 to 88.

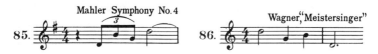

To be sure, in these four quotations the differences of the rhythmical events play a most vital part, as pointed out above under (2). Yet, disregarding these rhythmical events, the four motifs start with the same four tones, each time in a different order. If we replace their temporal succession by temporal coincidence, the variances vanish and the four melodic individualities concur in one harmonic identity:

Needless to say, the four tones harbor many, many more melodies.

From Ex. 85-88 we learn that a melodic line does not necessarily involve a change in harmony. It is obvious, however, that any change of harmony *necessarily* involves the formation of a melodic line, no matter how short, in the voice or tne voices which cause the harmonic change. This subject was extensively discussed in the preceding chapter on harmony, where it was revealed that the melodic progression of one or more voices of a harmony is conducive to the formation, we may say the creation, of ever new harmonies. Melodies, by combination, *integrate* into harmony. Ex. 85-88 show that the frame of a harmony is conducive to the formation, or creation, of ever new melodies. Harmony, by dissolution, *disintegrates* into melody. The two phenomena, melody and harmony, are linked, not closely, but inextricably together.

But short as our Ex. 85-88 are, they teach us much more.

Among the four equal tones of the several motifs* one of them (the tone *d*) appears, or let us cautiously say seems to appear, twice. This duplication is compulsory. For a motif composed solely of the constituents of a triad, which means *three* different tones, and yet embracing *four* tones in its melodic frame, has of necessity to repeat one of them. Yet this is a repetition only in a harmonic sense. In a melodic sense it is *not* a repetition; for melodically speaking the two *d*s are not the same.

While it is correct to say that the twelve tones of our chromatic scale exhaustively present the material of all their harmonic potentialities, it is not correct to say that they exhaustively present the material of all melodic potentialities

---

* The motif of Ex. 87 embraces *five* tones, the (real) repetition of the *g* in its second bar being one of its most essential formative elements. This item will be dealt with separately (page 120ff).

as well. We may acknowledge the multifariousness of harmonies drawn from the twelve tones of an octave; but we succumb to a grave fallacy if we apply the same consideration to melody — even setting aside all considerations of variety in interval successions or rhythmical events.

To begin with, the "twelve tones of an octave" do not embrace an octave but only a major seventh; the octave is the thirteenth tone and as such already a "repetition" of the first. And though it is entirely irrelevant *harmonically* whether we deal with any tone or with its higher or lower octave, it makes all the difference *melodically*.

If we replace the last tone of Ex. 86 by its higher octave, as shown in Ex. 89,

we do not even touch its harmonic frame. That remains exactly the same. But we distort the melody to irrecognizability. A painter might as well curve a line of a profile downward instead of upward and claim no change was made.

This is what would happen (Ex. 90a, b) to another Wagnerian theme (Ex. 91) if we squeeze its expressive gesture into the Procrustean bed of its harmonic frame:

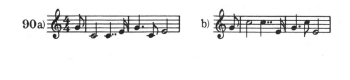

And with horror we may imagine the same procedure applied to another theme (Ex. 92) :

Mendelssohn, Octetto Op. 20

92.

In short, it is nonsense to marvel at the profusion of melodies that can be drawn from the "seven tones" of a scale, or the "three tones" of a triad, or the twelve tones available altogether. To equalize corresponding tones of different octaves, like d, d', d", d'" etc., in a melodic sense is as non-sensical as it would be to equalize the numbers 2,12,22,32 etc. From the melodic viewpoint the tone-gamut is unlimited, though only a limited discernible sector is in practical use, like the spectrum between the infrared and ultraviolet extremes. It is unlimited like the series of numbers, though, like this, it renews itself in periodic recurrence, the columns of tens in mathematics corresponding to the columns of octaves in music. But the melodic line, composed of the various absolute pitches (absolute according to their real vibration numbers) is not concerned with the fact that by mere accident, and solely for practical purposes, a certain periodic recurrence of names was agreed upon, just a such a recurrence of names was agreed upon in the series of numbers. We could just as well have given each number and each pitch a name of its own, except that this way things would have been harder to learn and to remember. Regardless of

any names whatsoever for its single constituents, it is the
pitch-line, its curve or curves, its shape, its profile, its ascen-
sions and descensions which determine the character, the
gesture of the melody — the challenge of Ex. 91, the tenderness of Ex. 86, the exuberance of Ex. 92.

Richard Strauss, in his "Symphonia domestica", draws
the last consequence of this consideration by entrusting the
violins with a note which is even below the range of the
instrument and therefore cannot be produced (Ex. 93).

The passage is reinforced by violas and horns and its
sounding thus assured. It would be intolerable, even to the
composer's *eye,* to replace the low *f♯* by its higher octave. He
wants the line at least to be understood — *playable or not.*
And so little does the composer trouble about its impracti-
bility that he does not even waste a syllable of explanation,
perhaps leaving some readers puzzled at the ostensible
"blunder".

The different melodic effect of a tone, or a series of
tones, in a lower or higher octave becomes especially manifest and attractive when both versions are juxtaposed within

an otherwise unchanged phrase (Ex. 94-96) :

(See also Ex. 298)

The adherence to either octave both times would completely destroy the very essence of the musical idea. Ex. 94 would lose the grave dignity of its announcement; the roguish turn of Ex. 95 would give way to a sodden dullness; while a dry repetition of the phrase in Ex. 96 would extinguish the charm of the melody, gracefully soaring away.

The two components of melody

It was said before that any temporal succession of pitches creates a melodic line, as contrasted with the temporal coincidence of pitches — harmony. It was further mentioned that there is a second point of contrast between melody and harmony, namely the rhythmic events which are completely irrelevant to the formation of harmony, yet most vital to the formation of melody.

In Ex. 97 we perceive such a melodic line, or pitch-line.

Yet it tells us little in the way of a real "melody". We would neither recognize nor enjoy it as such. We do both, however, as soon as the second component of melody, the rhythm, is added:

Beethoven, Violin-Sonata Op. 24

    Instantly the lifeless and shapeless frame takes on life and shape, and *beauty*.

    The mere pitch-line was a dead wax figure. Rhythm brought it to life. Rhythm became its breath, its soul.

    Thus we may roughly define melody as a definite succession of various pitches in a definite succession of rhythms. Such a rough technical definition will serve us for the present in the separate investigation of these two vital components of melody. Beyond this definition, however, and beyond this investigation which we are about to undertake, we must never lose sight of the fact that melody, like everything else under the sun, is much more than its analysis. We know we cannot exhaustively represent the nature of a tree by declaring it the sum of bark, branches, leaves and what not. The more we enjoy our power of improvement by technical knowledge, the deeper becomes our awareness of the mystery of origin both in nature and in art, our awareness of the unanswerableness of the ultimate questions.

If Ex. 97 showed that it is difficult to recognize a melody by the mere pitch-line divested of rhythm, Ex. 99-101 reveal that it is less difficult to recognize a melody by the mere rhythms divested of the pitch-line.

The notation of the pitches *instead* of their rhythmical patterns, as in Ex. 97, would certainly render Ex. 99-101 less suggestive of Beethoven's Fifth Symphony, Beethoven's Egmont Overture and Tchaikowsky's Fifth Symphony, respectively.

The rhythmical pattern is the actual backbone of the motif; it forms the real tie in the motivic structure and makes itself felt irrespective of tonal changes, be it in imitating voices (Ex. 102, 103)

Beethoven, 5th Symphony

or in the continuation of the line, as shown in Ex. 104, 105:

and later:

or, by an amazing coincidence*:

and later

---

* For the other item which links these two tunes so strikingly together we again refer to page 120ff.

Who on the other hand — to propose a counter-proof — would ever think of acknowledging any relationship between Ex. 106 and Ex. 107, though no less than the first ten tones of the pitch-line show complete conformity?

Following such observations, rhythmical patterns and pitch-line may be alternately substituted in a continuous chain. This practice need not and should not be confined to a game, but will prove a valuable training for the student of composition. He may start with a known theme, retain the tonal pattern while changing the rhythm, then retain the rhythmical pattern with a different pitchline and so forth. Or he may cast at random a tonal or rhythmical pattern as he would cast dice and start from there, alternately changing and retaining rhythm and pitch-line, respectively. Sometimes also known melodies may fit as intervening links of the chain. For example:

Retaining pitch-line, changing rhythm:

Retaining rhythm, changing pitches:

Same pitches, differently rhythmicized:

Same rhythm with different pitches:

Same pitch-line with different rhythms:

and so forth.

The individual metamorphoses from Ex. 108 to 113 show how the student can make the original motif travel through different styles and, in doing so, can draw a variety of inspirations.

Having divided melody into its two chief components, we will now give its first component, the pitch-line, a closer examination.

The simplest line is the straight line. A horizontal straight line would mean a melody which does not deviate from one pitch but keeps repeating this pitch, at least for a while. To compensate for the lack of tonal variety in such a case, other features would have to be added: varying rhythms, varying harmonies.

In Ex. 114 and 115 the melody repeats its pitch twelve times before leaving it.

The theme of Ex. 116 repeats its first tone no less than

thirty-four times before leaving it.

To be sure, the change of harmonies causes of necessity collateral melodic lines in the middle voices, so that the "line" of the upper voice makes itself felt only when it breaks its monotonous chant in bar 8. Yet, should we ascribe to this upper voice a merely harmonic function, we need but to leave it out (for this harmonic function is sufficiently performed in the *eb* of the lower octave) to see the injustice done to the composer's idea.

A straight line rising or falling at an angle to the horizontal would produce an ascending or descending scale.

Ex. 117 shows such a scale starting on the dominant of the key and carried through one and a half octaves.

The "melody" looks somewhat problematical. We know what it needs: the help of its other half, the rhythm. This added, we greet an old friend:

Chopin, Mazurka Op. 7 No. 1

118.

Here are a few more illustrations:

119.   Assai allegro   Beethoven, Sonata Op. 14 No. 2

120.   Adagio   Beethoven, String-Quintet Op. 29

121.   Scherzo   Beethoven, Piano-Trio Op. 97

In Ex. 121 the even flow of the line appears interrupted, "notched" as it were, at points where the will of the underlying *harmony* breaks through and makes the harmonical skeleton visible. We will frequently encounter such a contest of forces which results in the partial deflection of each of them, allowing none of them to assert itself unbrokenly.

The pattern of the descending scale shows in Ex. 122,
123:

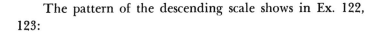

122.
Ca-ro no-me che il mio cor fe-sti pri-mo pal - pi - tar

123.

Copyright by Universal Edition, Vienna.
Reprinted by permission of Universal Edition & Associated Music Pub. Inc.

CHAPTER V

THE WAVE LINE

With the combination of ascending and descending scale-segments melody approaches its real nature: the *wave line* (Ex. 124-127).

The concept of the wave line taken in a wider sense will reveal the line's most frequent shape with its "ups and downs" not confined to stepwise motion but showing a variety of intervals (Ex. 128-132).

Permission granted by Jean Jobert, Paris, and
Elkan-Vogel Co., Inc., Philadelphia, Pa., copyright owners

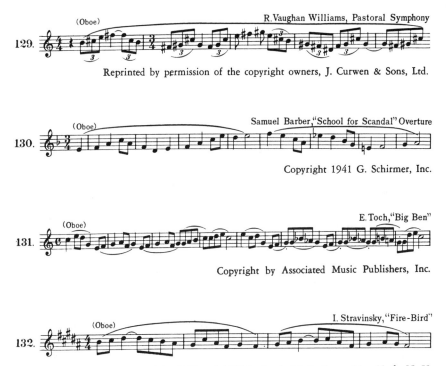

129. (Oboe) R.Vaughan Williams, Pastoral Symphony

Reprinted by permission of the copyright owners, J. Curwen & Sons, Ltd.

130. (Oboe) Samuel Barber,"School for Scandal" Overture

Copyright 1941 G. Schirmer, Inc.

131. (Oboe) E. Toch, "Big Ben"

Copyright by Associated Music Publishers, Inc.

132. (Oboe) I. Stravinsky, "Fire-Bird"

Copyright 1946 and 1947 by Leeds Music Corp., New York, N. Y.

It is at this point that a few principles appear to manifest themselves as more or less general and natural maxims among what to the fleeting glance may appear as arbitrary, haphazard melodical events.

If a melody is given time to develop on a broader basis, it shows that the smaller partial waves which constitute the whole line have the tendency to drive upwards their several highest tones (climaxes) until, after reaching the highest of these climaxes, the wave "breaks". The successive climaxes

add up, as it were, to one big wave, as marked by the dotted
line in the diagram.

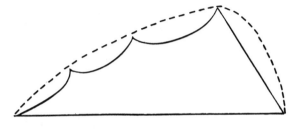

The climax of the last partial wave is at the same time
the climax of the melody. Ex. 133 and 134 illustrate these
observations.

About the climax of a melody we may say, *in general*:
The climax appears only once.

Its natural place is towards the end of the line, perhaps
in its last quarter or third.

If the melody, in the course of its line, approaches the
pitch of its last climax, it will either not reach this pitch, or
surpass it. Climaxes are exposed tones, and as such, tender
spots. We are sensitive to their repeated exposure. The ear
reacts to the exposure to sound as a photographic film reacts
to the exposure to light. An overdose of such an exposure has
in both cases a blurring effect on the sharpness of the line's
contour.

In order to demonstrate this point we will make a little
experiment with Ex. 133 by replacing one of its progressively rising climaxes by the repetition of another. (Ex. 135,
136, 137).

We feel the unsatisfactory effect of such distorted versions almost to the point of pain. The only possibility to
produce an effect which, though not reaching that of the
original, would still be tolerably satisfactory, would be to
avoid interfering at all with the sensitive pitch by decisively
avoiding its register, as shown in Ex. 138, 139.

It seems as though these characteristics of the melodic line — the single appearance of the climax, and its location near the end, between a long ascending and a short descending branch — would have their roots outside of music or art altogether in physical and psychical provinces.

In the progress of many natural phenomena similar conditions prevail. There are thunderstorms with a marked tendency to rise to mounting fury by comparatively slow degrees and to abate quickly after their most vehement outbursts. It is the pattern of many illnesses to develop slowly towards a "crisis", after which recession and reaction set in quickly. It is also the trend of slowly developing anxieties, fears and hopes to be quickly released after the materialization of their objectives. Finally, the phenomenon touches upon the physical-psychical borderland of our love-life.

These natural tendencies lie, metaphorically speaking, hidden in the work of art. The artist, in the process of creating his work, is not conscious of them. But his work is pulsation and manifestation of nature. Imbuing him, the man, nature imbues his work with her own features.

As the principle functions on a small scale in a defined melody — the germ of form — it functions as a formative element in a whole composition, as will be shown later in the treatment of Form.

Here are a few more illustrations, among which especially the long wide-curved lines of Ex. 140 and 143 foreshadow the influence on form of the above described qualities of a climax.

143. Andante moderato　　　　　　　　　　　　　　　Mahler, 2nd Symphony

144. (Flute)　　　　　　　　　　　　　　　　　Shostakovich, Symphony No. 1

145.　　　　　　　　　　　　　　　P. Hindemith, Violin-Sonata Op. 11 No. 2

It must be stressed that the tracing of such a principle is far from stating a law and far from attempting to cover the entire field. Its significance is the significance of any attempt at organization and order to the human mind. On principle, mammals live on solid ground; birds fly; fishes reproduce by spawning. Yet there are mammals which live in water, birds which do not fly, fishes which give birth to live young. These facts do not invalidate the principle. It holds good, no matter how frequently or how rarely it is controverted.

In merely apparent contradiction to the single appearance of the climax are cases where not only the exposed high pitch appears twice or three times but with it the whole phrase which includes it. In such instances the repetition of the climaxing phrase is an intended and well considered means to increase the rhetorical effect, as an orator would repeat a whole sentence to which he wishes to give special emphasis (Ex. 146-148).

148.

klopft mein lie - be - vol - les Herz, mein lie - be - vol - les

Herz, mein lie - be - vol - les Herz.

Melodic elasticity

If we subject the small partial waves of the big wave line to a closer examination, we observe that the changes of direction do not occur at random, but favor a certain tendency which may be expressed as follows:

A series of small steps in one direction is, *in general,* followed by a leap in the opposite direction.

Contrariwise, a leap in one direction is, *in general,* followed by a series of small steps in the opposite direction.

We may liken this characteristic to the tendency of a spiral spring which, if uncoiled and released, would snap back.

Ex. 149-155 show such melodic *elasticity,* the line rebounding after stepwise motion.

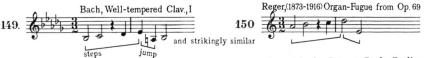

149. Bach, Well-tempered Clav., I

steps   jump

and strikingly similar

150 Reger,(1873-1916) Organ-Fugue from Op. 69

151. cu - jus a - ni - mam ge - men - tem.

152. glo - ria in ex - cel - sis De - o

153. triebst mich aus der letz - ten Frei - stadt

154. kratzt Pier - rot __ auf sei - ner Brat-sche

155. Et le re -tiens à mes __ ge-noux!

Ex. 156-171 show how a leap in the line is followed by stepwise motion in the opposite direction:

Mozart, Quartet K. No. 428

161.

(Note climax; see also page 67.)

Mozart, Quintet K. No. 516

162.

Schumann, Piano-Quintet Op. 44

163.

Mahler, 2nd Symphony

164.

ibidem

165.

Mahler, 8th Symphony

166.

Mahler, 8th Symphony

167.

(See page 92ff.)

Ex. 172 to 179 show melodic elasticity operating in a
chain of alternating directions.

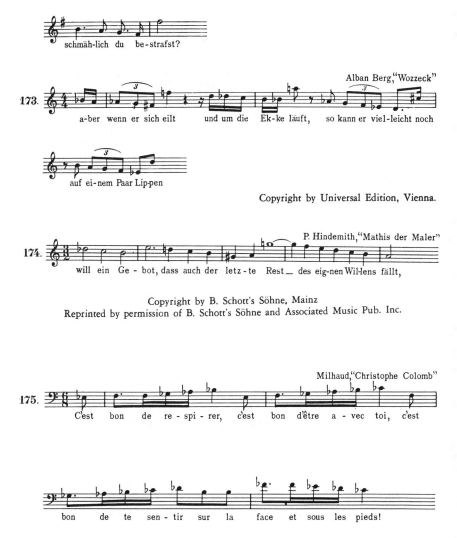

schmäh-lich du be-strafst?

Alban Berg,"Wozzeck"

173. a-ber wenn er sich eilt und um die Ek-ke läuft, so kann er viel-leicht noch

auf ei-nem Paar Lip-pen

Copyright by Universal Edition, Vienna.

P. Hindemith,"Mathis der Maler"

174. will ein Ge-bot, dass auch der letz-te Rest des eig-nen Wil-lens fällt,

Copyright by B. Schott's Söhne, Mainz
Reprinted by permission of B. Schott's Söhne and Associated Music Pub. Inc.

Milhaud,"Christophe Colomb"

175. C'est bon de re-spi-rer, c'est bon d'être a-vec toi, c'est

bon de te sen-tir sur la face et sous les pieds!

Copyright by Universal Edition, Vienna.
Reprinted by permission of Universal Edition & Associated Music Pub. Inc.

W. Walton, Symphony

176.

Carlos Chávez, "Spiral"

177.

W. Walton, Violin-Concerto

178.

Alois Hába, String-Quartet in quarter-tones Op. 7

179.

Occasionally the slopes of a wave will show subdivisions, notches or indentations, as it were, the lines assuming an indented shape as shown in the following diagram:

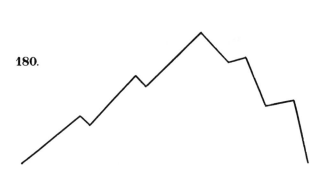

180.

These notches will function as small halting or resting places within the main trend of the line, their locations largely determined by harmonic influences. They will show either mere halts (Ex. 198), or repetitions of harmonically marked tones (Ex. 181, 182),

or small figures using neighboring tones for embellishment (Ex. 183, 184),

Mozart, Piano-Concerto K. No. 432

184.

(Note identity of structure!)

or even small recursions without prejudice to the principal direction. These latter will occur especially when the amplitude of the wave extends over a wider range, say beyond the interval of a tenth or so (Ex. 185-188). In such cases the notions "skip" and "step" assume a more relative meaning; within ranges as wide as those of Ex. 186 or 203, thirds and even an occasional fourth in the recoiling branch will still be felt as steps rather than as skips.

Chopin, Mazurka Op. 7 No. 1

185.

Chopin, Nocturne Op. 15 No. 2

186.

Beethoven, Violin-Sonata Op. 24

187.

(Compare also Ex. 167.)

Again the analogy with matters of form offers itself, as discussed on page 160.

The "wind-up"

If the wave starts with a skip, this skip is often preceded by a preparatory figure comparable to the motion we may make when getting ready for a throw—"winding up"—or for a jump—"taking a run". Such a preparatory figure will reveal a nervous, fidgeting character, a sort of wriggling before breaking loose; this character being produced by a group of short, quick notes, anything from a turn (mordent) to an independent, characteristic motif. The "winding up" motion is then followed by the "throw" or "jump", which in turn is followed by stepwise retrocession.

A few examples (189-197) may illustrate this feature.

(See also Ex. 134, bars 5 and 7; and Ex. 169, bar 2, where the feature is reduced to a mere suggestion, while wider leaps, such as in Ex. 193, 194 or 203, seem to call for a stronger preparatory effort.)

In Ex. 195-197 this figure, still clear in its preparatory function, takes on a more personal character:

The preceding illustrations show how both components of melody, pitch-line and rhythm, collaborate to produce the nervous, wriggling character of the winding-up figure, in that small tone-intervals (stepwise motion) combine with small time-intervals (quick rhythms).

In Ex. 168 and 169 such a figure appears reduced to a rudiment of two sixteenths, still strong enough to convey the impression. (Similarly: Ex. 255).

Harmonic influence in the way of "notches" makes itself felt in Ex. 197. Here the winding-up motion becomes part of the skip itself, as though a temperamental bowler would run along for a stretch, before releasing the ball.

However, this collaboration of the two components, pitch-line and rhythm, is not confined to such preparatory figures, but penetrates the elements of "elasticity", skips and steps, as well.

Here is how the feature of elasticity shows in either component of melody:

What constitutes "stepwise progression" in the linear component, namely a series of small *line divisions*, corresponds in the rhythmical component to a series of small *time divisions*—fast progression, short notes. What constitutes the "skip" in the linear component, namely the fusion of a few small tone divisions into one big tone division, corresponds in the rhythmical component to the fusion of a few small time divisions into one big time division—slow progression, long notes.

Usually linear and rhythmical elasticity go together: Skips are performed in slow rhythms, small steps in fast rhythms (Ex. 198-203).

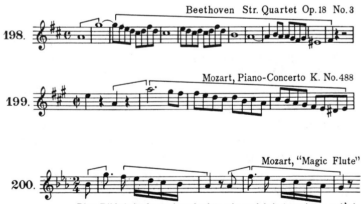

198. Beethoven Str. Quartet Op. 18 No. 3

199. Mozart, Piano-Concerto K. No. 488

200. Mozart, "Magic Flute"

Dies Bild-nis ist be-zau-bernd schön, wie noch kein Au-ge je ge-seh'n!

201. Wagner, "Lohengrin"

Nie sollst du mich be - fra - gen,

202. Mario Castelnuovo-Tedesco, String-Quartet

203. Hindemith, Quintet for Wind-Instrs., Op. 24 No. 2

The same correspondence is found in Ex. 141, 144, 153, 157, 159, 160, 162, 163, 164, 165, 166, 167, 168, 169, 170, 171, 172, 173, 174, 175, 176, 177, 181, 182, 185, 186, 188.

As to the skips, either both tones comprising them show slow progression (long notes), as in Ex. 153, 160, 163, 164, 166, 167, 171, 198, 202; or if the slow progression is confined to only one of them, it is usually the second, the one which *concludes* the skip; as though the line needed to catch its breath again after the exertion caused by the skip (Ex. 144, 156, 157, 162, 164, 167 (lower brackets) 168, 169, 170, 171, 172, 174, 176, 178, 185, 186, 190, 193, 196, 199, 200, 203, 208). Or else, the lapse of time may be produced or augmented by a rest, thereby still further increasing the impression that the line is panting for breath after the exertion of the skip (Ex. 166, 173 (!), 182, 183 (end), 184 (end), 195, 197, 204, 205, 209).

However, sometimes linear and rhythmical elasticity do not go together; i.e. elasticity may show only in one of the two components: either in the linear component alone (Ex. 149, 158, 161, 178, 179) or, in rarer cases, in the rhythmical component alone (Ex. 209).

If we give Ex. 204-209 a fleeting glance, we can **not** escape noticing the striking similarity of their structure.

A cursory first impression reveals as common features of their structure: (1) A starting segment of about four tones, marked by the seventh leap down. (2) A short rhythmical halt (or rest). (3) The "release", showing melodic elasticity of the last phrase.

To give the excerpts a common interpretation, just by feeling and impression:

A bunch of ants is dumped into a vessel (7th-leap down). Stunned for an instant (rest), they presently start scrambling up the walls.

Or:

Approach and occurrence of a collision (1). Numbed for a moment (2), everybody scrambles for safety (3).

Even the imaginary events of such interpretations suggest a sort of *psychical* elasticity, the accident not annihilating either ants or men, but causing increased activity and vitality.

Ex. 204-206 exhibit both linear and rhythmical elasticity in almost complete pureness. In Ex. 208 the elasticity in the rhythmical component of melody is somewhat stunted, while its counterpart, Ex. 209, shows elasticity confined only to the rhythmical component, the linear component yielding completely to the agency of harmony. In the double-fugue theme of Ex. 207 the feature splits into the rhythmical and linear component before our very eyes, the upper voice taking care of the linear half, unheedful of the rhythmical, the lower voice taking care of the rhythmical half, unheedful of the linear. The combination of the two voices produces the effect of both elements as though combined in a one-voiced melody, similar to Ex. 204, 205 and so many previous quotations.

CHAPTER VI

HOW HARMONY INFLUENCES MELODY

The more we proceed in our investigations on melody, the more we notice the influence of harmony on melody. Among the shaping forces in music, harmony and melody are the most closely related. To the superficial observer it may appear as though in the classical era harmony actually created melody, whereas in "modern" music melody actually creates harmony. But in reality this mutual impregnation is at work at all times, even though preponderance of one over the other may obtain at times. It is this mutual influence which incessantly promotes the evolution of each force, and with it, the broadening of each concept.

Ex. 210 shows clearly the melodization of harmony,

Mozart, "Eine Kleine Nachtmusik" K. No. 525

using the breaking of the two chief harmonies of the key for
the creation of a melodic line. Such patterns of broken harmonies permeate innumerable classical themes, the quotation
of which would fill books (see also Ex. 38, 92). Moreover,
this method permeates classical composition itself, showing
not only in the themes but also in accompanying and contrapuntal voices (Ex. 211, 212).

The use of "non-harmonic" tones breached the purity
of the classical harmony system. All non-harmonic, or foreign
tones (such as suspensions, appoggiaturas, anticipations, pass-
ing-, changing-, neighboring-tones, etc.) are invariably
melodic events. So, at bottom, are alterations (melodically
passing half-tones, foreign not only to the single harmony but
also to the key). Though this book does not share the tradi-

tional approach to harmony, as demonstrated at length in the respective section, we may as well use these current terms for convenience.

With regard to harmony the rhythmic, or metric, location of non-harmonic tones is of no consequence. They change the color of the harmony in a definite direction irrespective of their metric position.

With regard to melody, however, it makes all the difference whether a non-harmonic tone occurs in a metrically *accentuated* or in a metrically *unaccentuated* place.

Those nonharmonic tones which do *not* carry the metric accent have rather a playful, ornamental effect, leaving such melodies otherwise pretty close in character to the purely harmonic melodies (Ex. 213-216.)

Note the structural similarity of Ex. 213 to 215: The ascending tonic triad, its members all on accentuated beats, playfully surrounded by their neighbor-tones. Ex. 216 almost duplicates Ex. 215 in rhythm and in the placement of the harmonic and non-harmonic tones up to the half-cadence in bar 4, the only difference being the direction of the two lines.

However, if the non-harmonic tones carry the metric accent, that is if they appear on strong beats like suspensions and appoggiaturas, they give the melody a definite tint, esthetically and psychologically sharply contrasting with either purely harmonic melodies (such as Ex. 210) or with melodies using unaccentuated by-tones (such as Ex. 213-216).

The contrasting effect of accentuated and unaccentuated non-harmonic tones on the character of a melody is best illustrated if we juxtapose a representative of each type (Ex. 217, 218).

The constructive element of both melodies is a small, recurrent motif (indicated by ⌐⎯⎯⎯⏋) which consists of one tone of the underlying harmony preceded by a few non-harmonic tones. Ex. 217 reveals all the harmonic tones as accentuated, in the light; while the by-tones are accentless, weightless, in the shade, amounting to mere grace notes in character

and function. Ex. 218 reveals the harmonic tones as unaccentuated, in the shade, while the accents are invariably
carried by non-harmonic tones, suspensions in character and
function.

The masculine type and the feminine type

Melodies with unaccentuated, grace-note-like by-tones
form substantially one group together with the melodies that
consist of harmonic tones only, and we may put both varieties
under the common heading of harmonic melodies; while
melodies resting clearly on the use of accentuated, suspen-
sion-like non-harmonic tones, may briefly be called non-harmonic melodies.

Of the two sharply contrasting groups it can be said:

The psychological mark of the harmonic melody is di-
rectness, straightforwardness, simplicity, naturalness, manli-
ness, masculine strength.

The psychological mark of the non-harmonic melody is
veiledness, refinement, suspense, restraint, feminine tenderness, softness, the erotic touch ranging from tender yearning
to flaring passion.

The "manly" type of melody shows in Ex. 219-221.

It shows particularly in motifs of knights and heroes
(Ex. 261-264), in songs of masculine spirit such as marching,
drinking, hunting, fighting, patriotic songs (Ex. 222-235).

227. K. Wilhelm
Es braust ein Ruf wie Don - ner - hall,

228. Ludwig Fischer
Im küh-len Kel-ler sitz' ich hier auf ei - nem Fass voll Re-ben

229. Mozart, Don Giovanni
Finch' han dal vi - no cal - da la te - sta
u - na gran fe - sta fa pre - pa - rar.

230. Mozart, "Figaro"
Non più andrai far - fal - lo-ne a - mo - ro - so not - te e
gior-no d'in-tor - no gi - ran - do, del-le bel-le tur-bando il ri -
po - so, Nar - ci - set - to Adon-ci - no d'a - mor

The harmonic melody also expresses single-heartedness, artlessness, peace of mind (Ex. 236), nature, nearness to nature (Ex. 237-243) or to God (Ex. 244, 245), awe (Ex. 245), calm after the storm (Ex. 246, 247).

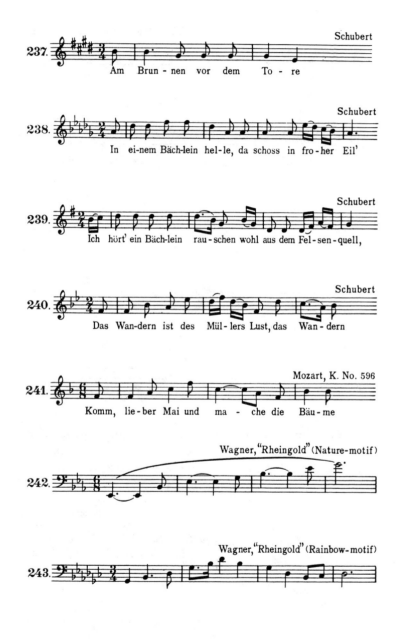

237. Schubert
Am Brun - nen vor dem To - re

238. Schubert
In ei-nem Bäch-lein hel-le, da schoss in fro-her Eil'

239. Schubert
Ich hört' ein Bäch-lein rau-schen wohl aus dem Fel-sen-quell,

240. Schubert
Das Wan-dern ist des Mül-lers Lust, das Wan-dern

241. Mozart, K. No. 596
Komm, lie-ber Mai und ma - che die Bäu-me

242. Wagner, "Rheingold" (Nature-motif)

243. Wagner, "Rheingold" (Rainbow-motif)

244. Si - lent night, ho - ly night, all is calm, all is bright.
Franz Gruber

245. *(Slow)* *Wagner, "Lohengrin"*
(Chorus) Wie fasst uns se - lig süs - ses Grau - en!
What mys - tic awe is o'er us stream - ing!

246. *Beethoven, 6th Symphony*

247. *Wagner, "Meistersinger"* (Watchman's song, End of Act 2)
Hört, ihr Leut', und lasst euch sa-gen, die Glock' hat eil - fe ge-schla-gen:
Hark to what I say, good peo-ple; e - le - ven strikes from each steep-le:

The "feminine" type of melody (Ex. 248-260), making
ample use of accentuated non-harmonic tones, is revealed in
themes of quiet, lyrical expression, in slow movements (Ex.
251, 252) or in passages of ebullient passion (Ex. 255).

248. *Mozart, Quartet K. No. 428*

Again it is the great psychologist Wagner who finds the most condensed expression, intensifying it still more by the interweaving of equally non-harmonic contrapuntal voices:

(Meistersinger)

256.

ibidem

257.

(Tristan and Isolde)

258.

(See Ex. 22, 23, also 370.)

And again we see the manly type, the harmonic melody, juxtaposed in sharp contrast:

264. (Tristan)

The knightly castle:

To be sure, the rhythmical component gives support to the psychic delineation: soft, flowing rhythms for the feminine type (256-260), clear cut, march-like rhythms for the masculine type, with a dash of squareness (263) or gallantry (261, 262, 264), respectively.

CHAPTER VII

DEFLECTIONS AND OTHER SPECIAL FEATURES

Related to the non-harmonic tones, and partly covering their appearance, is another feature of the melodic line which may be summed up under the heading of *deflection,* or *deviation.*

The deflection takes place either from the straight line (scale) or from the straight harmony (broken chord), in both cases irrespective of any metric position.

In Beethoven's Symphony No. 3 a glib version like Ex. 265 would easily suggest itself, the plain scale in bar 4 just filling the metric frame of the bar.

Instead, Beethoven writes:

Beethoven, 3rd Symhony

Compared with the neutral, colorless passage of Ex. 265 the animation and individualization of the line caused by the deflection is obvious.

Similarly he writes in his Fifth Symphony:

Beethoven, 5th Symphony

267.

It is interesting to know that his sketch-book, as edited by Nottebohm, shows the first shape of this theme as follows:

268.

Beethoven's correction makes it clear that he preferred the deflection even to the amenity of the suspension.

Deviation from straight harmony is evidenced in the countless "appoggiaturas" of classical melodies, such as Ex. 185, last bar, or Ex. 260.

The whole notes in Ex. 269 and 270 expose the harmonic skeletons of these lines:

269.

270.

Even where traditional harmonization, or tonality altogether, is denied, the line may still preserve its appoggiatura character (Ex. 271).

Eugene Goossens, Quartet No. 2

271.

The encircling approach

The melodic effect of the deflection is enhanced when both the low and high neighboring pitches, independent of their order, are used for appoggiaturas and thus form an *encircling approach* to the harmonic main tone before hitting it. (See Ex. 217, 218, 252, before and after each bar line, 256, beginning of bar 4, 257, beginning of bar 6, 259, over first bar line, 332, over second, fourth and sixth bar line, and others). The theme of Ex. 371 represents, in its second bar, a variant of particular piquancy, in that the encirclement is put, not before but after the main tone, g♯. Thus the encircling approach is turned, as it were, into a diverging withdrawal, bringing out still more plastically the deflection from the harmonic-melodic basis of the c♯ minor triad.

The effect of the encirclement can be further enhanced by extending the range of the appoggiatura beyond the immediate neighbor pitches, also by interpolating more than just one tone before reaching the harmonic pitch. The following quotation may serve as an illustration.

In bar 24 of Ex. 143 the last tone, *e*, has a strong tendency to proceed (resolve) to *f*. Yet the line deviates and forms an extended encirclement, a *loop,* as it were, around the harmonic tone, *f,* before reaching it, as indicated by the dotted lines (Ex. 272) :

G. Mahler, 2nd Symphony

272.

The intensifying, particularizing effect of the feature becomes apparent.

Deflections may occur in chains, in a manner similar to sequences. The line will then take on the appearance of a two voiced passage, the individual melodic fragments alternatingly continuing in two different registers (Ex. 273-276), either in parallel motion (Ex. 273 ⌐—ᴮ—¬, 274) or in opposite directions (Ex. 275, 276, 273 ⌊—ᴀ—⌋).

Bach, Well-temp. Clav. I, Fugue 24

273.

Alban Berg, Lyric Suite for Str. Quart.

274.

Even the deviation from the straight scale appears some-times in a chain, in that its subsequent steps are set up in two different octaves (Ex. 277, 278) :

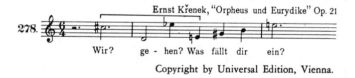

Ernst Křenek, "Orpheus und Eurydike" Op. 21

278.

Wir?   ge - hen? Was fällt dir   ein?

It obviously lies in the nature of this feature to counter-act the force of elasticity.

Iterances and elisions

On principle, a flowing melodic line will avoid the repe-tition of a pitch in too close a neighborhood, while its regis-tering effect on our mind is still alive; just as, in linguistic composition, the close recurrence of an expression affects us somehow unpleasantly and we prefer to substitute a syno-nym. The unpleasant effect, however, disappears as soon as we feel the repetition to be planted with deliberation and purpose. (Cf. the same idea in connexion with the climax, page 85.) So used, the fault becomes a virtue. In fact, the iteration either of one tone or of a small group of tones (figure, motif) in identical metric and rhythmic configuration forms a melodic trait of considerable consequence.

Such *iterances*, as we may call them, are of partly tonal, partly rhythmic nature. They may occur either in immediate succession (Ex. 279-290) or separated by short interruptions (Ex. 291, 293).

They create or increase the most diverse moods, produce and intensify the most multicolored imagery.

The effect of impish sprightliness in Ex. 279-283 is largely due to iterances.

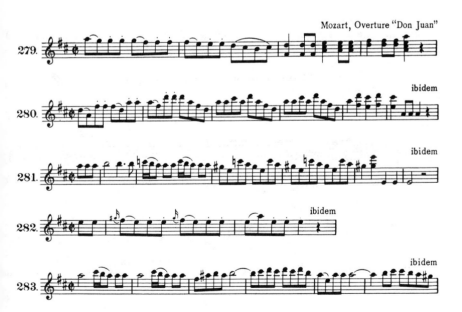

Iterances again give the special character to Ex. 284 and 285.

The popular "Fate" motif of Beethoven's Fifth Symphony (Ex. 108) would lose its significance if the three eighth notes were pitched in any other way than by merely repeating the same tone. This motif also shows how iterance elevates even the employment of no more than two different pitches to compelling pregnancy.

The same becomes clear from Ex. 286:

Iterance of one tone also shapes the motifs of Ex. 287 and 288,

while the characteristics of Ex. 289-291 rest on iterance of a
figure:

Copyright by Universal Edition, Vienna.

If we try to replace the iterances of Ex. 291 by sequences, as
in Ex. 292,

the face of the theme is gone, its individuality reduced to
staleness.

The first three bars of Ex. 293, compared with the first three bars of Ex. 195 reveal a remarkable similarity of structure.

Joseph Achron, First Violin-Sonata, Op. 29

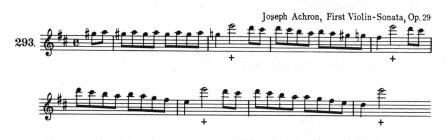

Here, as there: the beginning with the winding-up figure, made up of tone and by-tone iterance (bar 1), the leap upwards with ensuing rhythmical halt (bar 2), to be followed by a passage of tonal and rhythmic elasticity in bar 3. From here on the structures of the two quotations diverge. If we pursue Ex. 293 to its end, we see the iterances of bar 1 eclipsed by another iterance of far more telling effect: that of the loftily planted *e,* clinging doggedly to the pitch against all harmonic insinuations and hereby giving the theme its real clownish humor.

Iterances of the intermittent type sometimes take on the effect of what we may call a melodic fulcrum. The melody issues from a focal pitch (frequently but not necessarily the dominant) and returns to it repeatedly, moving either in one direction (Ex. 294-297)

or in opposite directions, which makes the fulcrum more a pivot or an axis (Ex. 298-302) :

As a counterfoil to iterances, melody sometimes shows the complete absence, the *emphasized* absence of any tone, so to speak "accentuated rests". Such *elisions* constitute wilful interruptions of phrases, and thus give a motif or a melody-section a striking rhythmical touch. Their logical place is in the beginning or in the middle of the phrase, always on downbeats, or at least on accentuated beats.

Ex. 303b and 304b show by comparison the effect of the elision, in contrast to the continuous line as appearing in 303a and 304a.

(Cf. also Ex. 149, 150, 166, 184, 195)

Especially marked is the "thematic rest" on the downbeat (Ex. 305, 306).

In polyphonic composition where the plasticity of the theme is of particular significance, elisions play an essential part (Ex. 307-309).

(Cf. also Ex. 183, 204, 209)

(Out of the 48 fugues of Bach's "Well-tempered Clavichord", 30 start with a rest on the downbeat of the first bar.)

Fugue themes are altogether the proper field for combined iterances and elisions (Ex. 310, 311).

Bach, Organ-Fugue

310.

William Schuman, "American Festival Overture"

311.

Copyright 1941 G. Schirmer, Inc.

(Cf. also Ex. 290, 291)

Though most effective in polyphonic style on account of the constant reappearance of the theme, the combination of iterances and elisions as a means of plastification holds its place in symphonic writing as well:

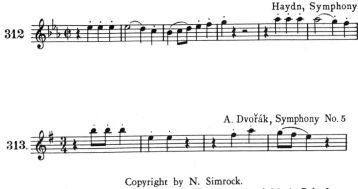

Haydn, Symphony

312.

A. Dvořák, Symphony No. 5

313.

An outstanding passage of combined iterances and elisions is presented in Ex. 314:

Note the frequency of the rests on the downbeats of bars 6-10 — *an iterance of elisions.* What chords could match these rests in eloquence and impressiveness? The deep rifts precisely on these downbeats are a thematic resource of highest expressive power. The very absence of any sound constitutes an audible effect of contrast, comparable to the visual effect of the blank spots the etcher or silhouettist would use for constrast. Bars 10-13 represent a kind of a stretto in which rests as well as chords form iterances, opposing each other in a struggle for predominance. Halting all harmonic or melodic progressions, this exciting passage rests entirely on the effect of iterances and elisions.

COUNTERPOINT

"... that action and counteraction which from the reciprocal struggle of discordant powers draws out the harmony of the universe"

Edmund Burke, "Reflections on the Revolution in France"

CHAPTER VIII

THE MEANING OF COUNTERPOINT

Perhaps it is the somewhat cryptic term itself which accounts for the fact that, among all the branches of the "gray theory" of music, counterpoint sounds the most theoretical, the most scientific, the most cryptic. The innocent layman would rather link the term to higher mathematics or physics than to a thing as live, serene and lovely as music. Just as melody must be a matter of sheer inspiration, probably counterpoint is a matter of sheer speculation — the one as close to nature as the other far from it.

Theory derives the term from "punctum contra punctum", or "point against point", adding that "punctum" once had the meaning of a musical note and therefore counterpoint means "note against note". This explanation is supposed to be very old, going back to the first attempts at singing in several parts. Just exactly which learned personage is responsible for this explanation, seems to be another mystery; nevertheless it is adhered to religiously and deferentially up to the present day and it certainly leaves us none the wiser.

In the first place, notwithstanding the historic origin of the term, the real nature of counterpoint is anything *but* "note against note", even in strict sixteenth century counter-point where such application would cover only the first of the redoubtable "five species"—the one which *in practice* hardly played any role at any time. Besides, does it not seem rather far-fetched to bring the *second* "point" into the definition at all? Does—or did at any time—"afternoon" mean *"noon* after noon"? Does "undertaker" mean *"taker* under taker"? Why then must counterpoint mean *point* counter point? Finally, if "punctum", or "point", had at one time the connotation of a musical note, it surely had *at all times* the meaning of *topic* or *subject.* And while the ancient interpretation seems to accentuate the "point" part, we definitely prefer to shift the emphasis to the "counter" part of the term. This makes counterpoint simply the *point of contrast;* and the only reason why such a simple explanation is nowhere to be found must be that it would make things too easy, and would deprive the term of its scientific aura.

Suppose a stage play should start by showing a loving couple happily embracing one another, and from the wings, left and right, should enter the respective parents and give their blessings, and then the curtain should fall again. We certainly would revolt at such preposterousness. What we would miss, and eagerly demand to see, is the various happenings *in point of contrast.*

A meeting of any kind will hardly take its course with every one nodding assent to the speaker's discourse and leaving thereafter. Rather, it will produce a discussion *in point of contrasting ideas*, voicing the pros and cons, and thus resulting in clarification and final shaping of the issue. Herein lies the virtue of the "healthy opposition": it becomes a means not of obscuration but of clarification, not of obstruction but of propulsion.

Apply these considerations to music and you get the real, intrinsic meaning of counterpoint, one of the most powerful *shaping forces in music;* we might even go so far as to say, one of the most powerful shaping forces in art altogether.

When in Wagner's "Meistersinger" the crowd of Nuremberg citizens comments on Beckmesser, one group ridiculing his pitiful appearance while another group is still impressed by his high civic rank, the opposition of the two groups obtains musical support by the contrapuntal treatment of the passage (Ex. 315):

Scheint mir nicht der Rech - te!   An der Toch-ter Stell' ich   den nicht möch-te!
Is - n't   he   a   fat   one!   In the la - dy's place I'd   not   have that one!

Witz!   Der hat im   Ra - te Stimm' und   Sitz!
prate!   He   is   a   learn - ed ma - gi - strate!

(English version by H. & F. Corder)

Thus the example illustrates in a *double* way, by word and tone, the nature of counterpoint: opposition, contradiction, fighting. The two opposed musical lines reveal the chief weapons of this fight, the two chief means of contrapuntal expression: Contrast in rhythm and contrast in the direction of movement. When one voice is in repose, the other moves on; when one voice moves up, the other moves down.

If the words were spoken in their exact rhythms instead of sung, at least one of these fundamentals of counterpoint, rhythmical contrast, would still be distinctly felt.

The above considerations make it clear that, rather than "note against note", counterpoint means the simultaneous presence of two (or more) contrastingly *moving* voices, or as we may say, *melodic lines.*

As such the musical phenomenon of counterpoint is familiar to us from countless experiences. Let us now, for further investigation, single out one of those familiar acquaintances:

Bach, Two Part Invention

316.

Bar 1 of Ex. 316 shows a moderately fast motion with upward moving tendency. Imitated in the lower voice in bar 2, the upper line now puts up a typical counterpoint against the lower one: distinct rhythmical contrast, distinct downward motion. The same procedure repeats in bar 3, with the order of the voices reversed. Bar 4 keeps only to one of the fundamentals of counterpoint, namely the rhythmical contrast. So does bar 7 again, while bars 5 and 6, in absolute parallelism both rhythmically and tonally, completely upset the sacred "rules" of counterpoint. The same happens almost throughout the whole of bar 9.

Is it, then, that Bach did not know even the fundamental rules of counterpoint? Or was he just negligent when writing these "false" bars, or did he do it for mere mischief and spite, "pour épâter le bourgeois", as the French say?

We cannot deny that the piece is utterly charming, including, *to say the least,* these wrong bars.

Two children play at catch, or hide and seek, the pursued every once in a while teasing the pursuer in a demonstrative challenge.

Two butterflies are engaged in a flirtation, chasing each other, yet once in a while flying together for a stretch in a coquettish mock-truce, until one breaks loose again and provokes the other into resuming the chase.

By slackening the tension of "counterpoint" for a short while these arraigned bars render the ensuing resumption of the chase the more effective. The unexpected cessation of the intrigue becomes an intrigue in itself, like the feinting retreat of a fencer. The passage takes the effect of counterpoint *inside* of counterpoint; opposing the opposition, contradicting the contradiction.

So strong is the effect of this feature that it holds good even in the rigorous structure of a fugue, consolidating the parallelism to its limit, the unison:

Bach, Well-temp. Clav. I, Fugue X

At the bottom of this feature lies the principle that any quality is apt to weaken and to lose its effect after a while; and the best preventive for that is an offsetting and reanimating intermission. This observation touches upon the basic "tension—relaxation" principle of form, as treated in the following section.

However, this is not the only point which links counterpoint with form, in fact makes counterpoint a powerful functional agent of form.

CHAPTER IX

ORNAMENTAL AND FERMENTATIVE COUNTERPOINT

Counterpoint does not always exhibit the same appearance and function. We may discriminate between two main trends of counterpoint which not only differentiate its quality and nature but also have a bearing on its evolution.

In external appearance the difference may perhaps be best described by the fact that the one type is principally based on close thematic or motivic unity of the opposing voices, while the other type does not keep to such unity but either slackens it considerably or drops it altogether. The first kind represents the *imitative* type, covering the epoch of polyphonic writing which climaxes in canon and fugue. Here counterpoint has a predominantly ornamental function; ornamental in a broad sense, as an architectural designation and with no prejudice to the personal depth of the composer or the profundity of contents of the composition. The other type of counterpoint spurns the ornamental quality and favors a function which we may rather describe as stirring, or *fermentative*. With respect to formative power we may say that the ornamental type of counterpoint is to a lesser degree a shaping force than the fermentative type is.

Ornamental counterpoint, the altogether prevailing form of expression during the hey-day of polyphonic writing, became the theater of a particular technical skill. It is, up to the present day, the only type of counterpoint with which traditional study deals. Though a source of utter delight in the hands of a real tone-*poet* like Bach or Mozart, it carries the danger of degenerating into an idle sport or, worst of all, into dry pedantry—"paper-music". If, before attempting to write a fugue, we would take the trouble to investigate, we would find that Bach almost never carries the first appearance of a theme throughout a whole fugue, and that he constantly keeps applying far-reaching changes to his themes and counter-themes. We would thus become more conscious of dealing not with a skilful technical routine but with tone-poetry which just happens to employ the preferred idiom of the period.

Fermentative counterpoint escapes the danger of pedantry to a great extent by being based on continuous free, inventive creation which shields the composer from the traps of technicalities.

The real originator and great professor of fermentative counterpoint is Richard Wagner.

Small wonder that the expert professors declared his way of using—abusing, rather, in their eyes—the hallowed craft rank dilettantism. They were at least not wrong in sensing that this kind of counterpoint, though still undeniably felt as counterpoint in the sense of contrastingly moving voices, was a different art from what counterpoint used to be hitherto by its very nature. For this very nature was definitely of the ornamental type, worshipping at the shrine of imitation and therefore clinging to the texture of tight motivic unity. Even where Wagner approaches the ornamental type, as in the mock-fugue (bar 138ff.) or the three theme stretto (bar 158ff.) of the "Meistersinger" Prelude, it is as though he would frivolously flirt with the austere craft, would nod a lofty, insulting "hello" to the redoubtable academy. For the rest of this piece, however, almost throughout it from beginning to end, the contrapuntal treatment discards the principle of dense motivic unity, the imitative style, and replaces it with the principle of motivic independence, of freely progressing, continuously renewing "infinite melody". Counterpoint takes on a new, strong, individual function: it becomes the leaven, the ferment, the very *stuff of fermentation;* it acts as the agent of promotion, propulsion, *formation.* At the same time it changes the character of the music from spiritual lucidity to brewing emotionalism.

The limits of this book do not permit the reproduction of a piece of such dimensions as would be necessary to demonstrate all this in detail. It is strongly recommended that one listen attentively and repeatedly to a good recording of the entire Prelude, alternately with and without the use of a score.

So strongly is the difference of the two types of counterpoint felt, that passages like the two mentioned above (bar 138ff. and bar 158ff.), by their mere approach to ornamental counterpoint, have, in their environment, a similarly relaxing effect to that which the passages of parallelism in Ex. 316 and 317 have in their environment of ornamental counterpoint. Parallelism is to ornamental counterpoint what ornamental counterpoint is to fermentative counterpoint.

Bach and Wagner represent the chief exponents of music which is essentially rooted in polyphonic conception, or counterpoint; ornamental or fermentative, respectively. Their music does not *apply* counterpoint; it derives its very life and breath from it. Between them, temporally as well as ideologically, lies the type of music represented in the symphonic style of the eighteenth and nineteenth century, which attempts to combine homophonic and polyphonic writing and to reconcile both basic concepts.

The great exponent of this style is Mozart. With him too, as with Bach and Wagner, counterpoint is not an accessory, but an *intrinsic part* of the creative mechanism. Yet, going through the alembic of his mind, counterpoint again takes on an individual quality and function. Both Mozart and Wagner are true disciples of Bach; but by dint of their strong personalities the common tool, counterpoint, is bent and shaped in the directions their individual minds work. And it appears that while Wagner's counterpoint becomes functional towards *fermentation* and—in the wake of it— *emotionalism,* Mozart's counterpoint, directed the opposite way, becomes functional towards *crystallization,* serenity and *spiritualism.*

A few bars—Ex. 318 and 319—may reveal these respective qualities in a condensed form, as in a microscopic bloodtest, so to speak. Ex. 318 shows bars 67 to 75 of Wagner's "Meistersinger" Prelude, Ex. 319 bars 58 to 67 of Mozart's Overture to "The Magic Flute".

Counterpoint, the agent of fermentation: Wagner

Counterpoint, the agent of crystallisation: Mozart

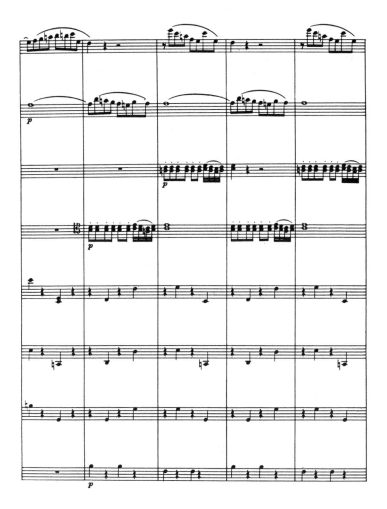

The excerpts also show how the respective orchestrations underline the two contrasting functions of counterpoint. The Mozartean use of counterpoint combines with the preservation of pure, unadulterated sound-colors towards crystallization and cool spirituality. The Wagnerean use of counterpoint combines with the creation of alloyed, blended sound-colors towards fermentation and intoxicating sensuality.

Thus counterpoint infiltrates even orchestration; its diverging tendencies duplicate in orchestration.

Apart from these observations, it becomes clear that counterpoint is just as much subject to constant evolution and flux as is melody and harmony, with which it is indissolubly interwoven.

If Bach, Mozart and Wagner are three individual masters of counterpoint, they are wellnigh masters of three individual arts.

Intrinsic and integrant as counterpoint is with these composers, it still does not constitute so elementary a musical factor as do for instance melody and harmony, without which hardly any kind of articulate music is conceivable. The participation in the use and development of contrapuntal writing is to a high degree an individual and personal matter among composers. It in no way belittles the value of Debussy's, Puccini's or Johann Strauss' works that their minds did not primarily work in the direction of contrapuntal thinking.

And yet, the idea of counterpoint is apt to tint even a musical inspiration of the most unsophisticated nature.

If Strauss writes:

the little superimposed figure is certainly neither relative to
the melody nor to the accompaniment. What it indicates is a
last rudimentary trace of counterpoint, still clearly showing
its characteristics of rhythmical contrast and contrary motion.

FORM

"*The very essence of life is movement*"

Jack London, "*The Sea Wolf*"

CHAPTER X

THE BASES OF FORM

Whatever FORM may be, let us not confuse it with *forms,* namely, the forms used in classical music. These forms generally constitute what is taught and studied under the heading of "form", frequently augmented by "analysis", though the "analysis" also means nothing else than the analysis of these forms. This study will enable one to tell whether a piece of the classical period is written in the form of Sonata, Rondo, Variation, etc.

But if a composer for any reason would like to break away from them, and, at the same time, *the forms* are the only thing he knows about FORM, he must necessarily feel pretty much lost. And if a student who knows all the terms and what they stand for is confronted with a piece of music that happens to follow none of these standard models, all his knowledge of form plus analysis will be of no avail to him. Does this mean that such a piece has no form at all?

Besides, what is the form of a Prelude, a Fantasy, a Nocturne, a Berceuse, a Kyrie, a Love Duet? And for that matter, what is the form of most of our contemporary "Sonatas" or "Symphonies", in spite of their traditional titles?

A piece may be written in any one of the classified forms to its minutest detail and still may exhibit a pitifully poor FORM.

And a piece may reveal not the slightest affiliation to any of the traditional forms, and yet may be a prodigious master-piece of FORM.

FORM is to forms as the universe is to a mountain or a tree.

How would you describe the form of a fugue? Among the wealth of Bach's fugues no two show the same structure. Yet each of them displays a masterly FORM, be it macrocos-mically majestic or microcosmically graceful and dainty.

In highest art content and form coincide. How, then, could FORM be reduced to a few forms when content is limited only by the universe?

True, in the heyday of classical music, most of it was written in the traditional forms, mainly the sonata form. This was comparatively new and young; it was a good frame, firm enough and yet flexible enough; and it had evolved *for good reasons,* as had the smaller and lighter forms, too. The great masters did not need to bother further about these forms, for they had plenty to say, plenty to fill the frames anew and anew with their original, personal ideas; so much so that they unwittingly kept contributing to their further development, modifying them, deflecting them, bending them under the will of their individual genius. For the small talent, however, they were just welcome vehicles, easy tracks to follow, apt to turn FORM into formalism and pedantry. And what else but formalism and pedantry is it if theory keeps teaching analysis of the few forms? Is it a worthy goal to the creative mind to know that this piece is written in sonata form, that in rondo form? *Who cares?* Surely not the composer. Surely not the performer. Surely not the audience.

Research should not stop at describing some surface appearances and putting tags and labels on them. Nor will such knowledge ever help a creative talent to express himself musically.

It was said above that composition of the past arrived at some forms, or frames, *for good reasons.* Let us try to investigate these reasons instead of the forms; the sources and forces at work below the surface, instead of the surface. And let us see if these forces do not apply to composition at large, beyond the frames developed so far.

The meaning of form

Schopenhauer calls architecture "frozen music". This is not merely an aesthetic comparison; the analogy goes into the very substance of both arts. By the same token one could call music "sounding architecture". The "measure" is essential for both to such an extent that music borrows the very term for its metrical units. Architecture in turn uses the "motif", another kind of unit, as a germ-cell for building purposes—just as music does—by reiteration, modification, combination, grouping and regrouping. Perfect FORM crowns the masterpiece of architecture as well as the masterpiece of music.

Yet, while architecture unfolds itself in the medium of *space,* the medium in which music unfolds itself is *time.*

Concentrating on the subject of music, let us consider the qualities and characteristics of time.

Time rolls on uniformly, uninterruptedly, unceasingly. Units add to units, to form bigger units, unceasingly. Seconds accumulate to minutes, to hours, to days, weeks, months, years, decades, centuries. At the bottom of time operates a monotonous rhythm, mirrored in our own being by the beat of our heart, the pulsation of our bloodstream.

This regularly reiterant rhythm forms, as it were, a bottommost stratum of which we become conscious only at rare intervals.

Above this nethermost stratum lies and works another stratum: the periodical alternation of contrast.

While seconds, minutes, hours roll on in constant equality, at the same time there is a constant alternation of day and night, winter and summer, low tide and high tide. While the fundamental rhythm of pulsation accompanies us continuously, at the same time we alternate in exhalation and inhalation, in the consciousness of being awake and the unconsciousness of sleep.

It is the interplay of these two elementary forces that builds and feeds the skeleton of music. Primitive music may be satisfied with the basic element, the rhythm. The reiteration of a definite rhythmical pattern, produced mainly, if not solely, by percussion instruments, will create a certain stirring effect. Inspired by bodily movements, and inspiring bodily movements, like marching or dancing, it may be protracted at random, may give suitable support to such performances, may create certain moods and even a kind of primitive mental ecstasy. But it will never create *musical form,* no matter how complicated, intricate and refined such rhythmical patterns may be. For that, the second element has to be added: the element of *contrast,* of black and white, of light and shade, of *tension and relaxation.* It is the right distribution of light and shade, or of tension and relaxation, that is formative in every art, in music as well as in painting, sculpture, architecture, poetry.

In the development of musical form the force of contrast, the alternation of tension and relaxation, more and more restrained the primordial force of the rhythmical pulsation to the background, to the undermost stratum, keeping it there, as it were, tamed and subdued. And though the interplay of the two forces will always have its bearing on form, we may, in the interest of terseness, confine ourselves to the definition of FORM as the *balance between tension and relaxation*.

The more equilibrated this balance is, the better will be the form of a musical piece. Thus it becomes clear that form will always be largely a matter of feeling, not to be pinned down like the signature of a key or the *established forms*. Yet, this feeling for form can be aroused, developed and fortified in the student of composition. It must be stated here, however, that when we speak of balance we by no means mean a half and half distribution of the contrasting elements. On the contrary, as we will soon see, the proportion, if expressed in measuring terms, will always favor the tension segment as against the relaxation segment.

In Ex. 321 a rhythmical pattern of four bars is sounded four times in succession:

321. "The Lorelei" (Fr. Silcher, 1838)

Apart from the last repetition in which bar 2 shows a slight change (♩ ♪ instead of ♩·), the pattern keeps repeating without any change (Ex. 322):

322. 1) ♪| ♩·♫ ♫♫ | ♩·   ♩ ♪| ♩· ♪♫♫ | ♩·͜♩

2) ♪| ♩·♫ ♫♫ | ♩·   ♩ ♪| ♩ ♪♫♫ | ♩·͜♩

3) ♪| ♩·♫ ♫♫ | ♩·   ♩ ♪| ♩ ♪♫♫ | ♩·͜♩

4) ♪| ♩·♫ ♫♫ | ♩ ♪♩ ♪| ♩ ♪♫♫ | ♩·͜♩

The third phrase, by ascending to the key of the dominant and resting (cadencing) on it temporarily, creates a certain tension, as though a weight should be lifted and should accumulate potential energy, eager to be released again. This release back to the previous level (the tonic of the key) takes place in the following (fourth) phrase—the relaxation after the tension. Or, the effect of phrases 3 and 4 may be compared to the bracing effect of our inhalation and the relaxing effect of our exhalation, respectively.

Should we stop the melody at the end of the third phrase, we would intensely feel the "call" of the tonic, g— its power of attraction. The harmonic-melodic figure of the accompanying middle voices here (bar 4 of the third phrase) gives distinct support to this "home-calling" tendency. It works as a bridge, preparing and heralding the following section with all its implications. These joints have a particularly delicate task and function in FORM, as we will soon see.

From the viewpoint of the theory of *forms*, Ex. 321, on account of its structure and its measurements, is a specimen of what is termed the "two-part song-form", and that is that.

From the viewpoint of FORM the little song reveals, in the nucleus, the interplay of the undercurrent forces that make for FORM, *any form,* regardless of measurements and their resulting terms, regardless of epoch and style; just FORM as an artistic vessel, or garment of musical expression —in short, composition.

It was mentioned before that the definition of FORM as the balance between tension and relaxation does not imply an equal ratio of the sections devoted to each of the two elements, but that in mere temporal extent the former preponderates over the latter. That, too, shows in the little form of Ex. 321, where only the last quarter of the song, phrase 4, covers the relaxation part. It would be wrong to believe that the tension part, taking place in phrase 3, is equal in length to the relaxation part. For as stated above, the creating motive for both is the rising to the dominant (D major) and the falling back to the tonic (G major). But without the preceding phrases 1 and 2, the key of G major would not be established; without the key being established, phrase 3 could not be felt as a *rise* to its dominant, nor phrase 4 as a return to it, and therefore the tension-relaxation effect must collapse. (By the same token the sounding of the high *g*, in both phrases 1 and 2, is the premise of the climax of the melodic line, the high *b*, in its last quarter and close to its end). Thus the portion of the ascent, both in form and melodic line, outweighs the portion of the descent considerably.

Larger forms

A side-glance at the construction of a drama will help to illustrate and interpret this phenomenon. The drama, too, unfolds itself through the medium of time, and uses the mechanism of logical and psychological consecution. Here a plot is created, developed, lifted from level to level by continuously added intrigues, the ascending line covering the predominant portion of its range; until in the last (often short) act, the intricate threads disentangle, and no superfluous wordiness hampers the precipitation to the end.

The comparison with the drama, though applicable as an overall principle to small forms like Ex. 321, intensifies with the larger musical forms. As the drama will not roll on uninterruptedly, but subdivide into smaller sections—acts, scenes—so the larger musical form, even if still in one movement, will provide, by subdivisions, for resting points and breathing spaces. And while the short descending line will be relatively straight and taut, the long ascending line, ascending as a whole, will show curves, notches, retarding moments, similar to those of the melodic line (Ex. 134). A tragedy will not loosen its grip after the climax; but before it, on the long way up to it, provision might well be made for some temporary, refreshing laughs. They will help the reader or spectator to brace himself for the ever tightening grip of the plot; and interspersed as welcome little spots of contrast, they will prevent the interest in the main problem from flagging and tiring. In the same way a light comedy, straight to the point after the climax, will benefit by weaving into the ascending section an occasional musing contemplation or a similar incidental excursion into the more serious and weighty.

In musical form these little contrasts within the main trend are not felt as impairing the drive; on the contrary, they set it off to better advantage, giving each section a new impetus.

A masterpiece of form will reveal these qualities even though it may follow none of the classical forms and may therefore deny any traditional approach of formal analysis.

Listen to a good recording of Wagner's "Meistersinger" Prelude; first let it just affect you, then listen again with a score or piano-score.

The almost constantly ascending line covers the overwhelmingly major part of the piece, up to bar 211. The following diagram (Ex. 323) may illustrate its periods of tension and relaxation. The numbers refer to the respective bars, and the idea is to mark these bars in the piano score before reading it together with a recorded or live performance.

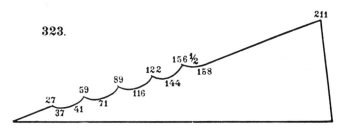

323.

The ascending fragments of the line tend to preserve the key (C major) and the pushing, driving, vigorous, masculine character. The receding fragments provide the change of mood (lyrical, feminine in bars 27-37, 89ff; grave, impressive in 59ff; humorous, mocking in 122ff) which is also largely supported by change of key.

With the exception of the sudden change at 122, the indentations do not appear as pronounced as in the diagram; rather they are softened by smooth modulations and occasional bridges (37-41, 89-97). A constant undercurrent of moving contrapuntal voices, often supported by or resulting in massed, tension-charged harmonies, keeps driving, urging, rolling the masses like molten metal in the process of founding, and constantly building, building, building. Each of the mounting fragments marks the achievement of a higher level, until, in a broad, last, irresistible sweep (158-211) a gigantic, crushing climax is reached, triumphant like the hoisting of the victorious flag in conquered territory. From this peak, the piece plunges to its end in a few bars.

Wagner was often accused of making a hodgepodge, a potpourri of the themes contained in his operas, for their respective overtures. In "Rienzi" he still kept to the traditional overture in the sonata form. But feeling somehow restrained in his personal ideas by this—or probably any—traditional form, he created his own form and mastered it. True, he used the themes of the opera for material. But why should such material be less fit for perfect form, if tamed and subjugated by the master's hand? And if it is true that in highest art. content and form coincide (which means that inspiration creates its own form) it is equally true that form as a tool—self-created or accepted—retroactively can have an inspiring effect on the artist, as even the mere objective tool may have—the blank manuscript paper, canvas or marble block.

So in a piece like the "Meistersinger" Prelude, form is neither a loose potpourri nor just the "grouping of a given thematic material", as the notion of form is frequently defined. Irregular and unruly in every detail as it seems to be, akin nowhere in detail or *in toto* to any of the traditional forms, its form is compellingly, irresistibly, inescapably present—omnipresent, *sovereign,* responding in the highest degree to *the shaping forces in music.*

A promise is given in the beginning of the piece which is magnificently fulfilled in the end. A goal is set up which, approached step by step in constant onward drive, is gloriously reached. We set out in venturesome youth and, seasoned by the events of the journey, we return wise and mature.

In such interpretations by way of feeling and touch, we may approach such nondescript, yet ever so present form. At the same time, while none of the traditional forms is catalogued by this approach, a most important basic principle is revealed: The principle of *tripartition.* To it most of the forms can be traced, regardless of their substructures, proportions, standards, terms.

It is of little concern whether we call the three parts exposition, development and reprise, or the sections of the three-part song-form, or Menuetto, Trio and da Capo, or just A B A^1. The affinity and correlation of the flanking parts will always be felt as against the middle part, the bearer of intensification, plot, *contrast.* Whence we came, thither we return, after all the blooming and climaxing, after all the turbulence and trepidation. The principle of tripartition, as manifest in art, is rooted in nature, in our souls, in our very existence.

And here is where the "formless" Meistersinger Prelude touches classical form—in the high-levelled, if epitomized, reprise and coda (measure 188 to the end) of its missing "Sonata".*

It is easy enough to see that the principle of tripartition also applies to a piece as small as Ex. 321. Phrases 1 and 2 obviously make up one coherent part, as against phrase 3, the contrasting middle part, and phrase 4, the reprise. Flatly, there is no such a thing as a two-part song-form. What makes song-form as such the prototype of the tripartite form, is simply the presence of a contrasting middle section between two analogous flanking sections, irrespective of any number of bars or any other tabulations. To divide song-form into one two-part, and one three-part song-form is like dividing the family of dogs into a group of dogs with four legs, and a group of dogs with a wart on the left jowl.

Small as the curve of the little phrase 3 (Ex. 321) is, it deserves all the interest and all the credit for bringing about FORM. Here, in this middle section of the song-form, is the place for the tension so essential for good form.

The following example may illustrate how high this curve, scarcely more than an indication in Ex. 321, may bulge and vault in the master's hand to result in utterly delightful, masterly form.

---

* It may be mentioned here that the term "Sonata" originally meant nothing else than played music, instrumental music, *musica sonata* as contrasted to sung music, vocal music, *musica cantata*.

Allegretto — Schubert, Menuetto from Octetto Op. 166

The composer could easily have satisfied the academic requirements by entering the reprise after the half-cadence in bar 18. The modulation back to the tonic was consummated, nothing was in the way of the return.

Instead, what happens? Ignoring the easy path, the passage swerves to a remote key and from there, traveling through ever new keys (25-33) soars high up, to land again on the dominant (bar 33) and to enjoy now, *only now,* the infinitely more gratifying reprise.

And while we are on the subject: Again it would have been easy to make the conventional reprise, perhaps concluding it in the main key by merely transposing the last four bars (9, 10, 11, 12) into F major. Nothing of the kind happens. First of all the theme itself is diverted right after the first pair of bars. And now, like a faint reverberation of the preceding surge, the tide again rises in threefold sequence (38ff) until it breaks upon the unexpected D major triad (43). Nonplussed, as it were, the passage turns back and, groping about in utmost tenderness, floats down, and, finally, *only now,* home.

What is this? An "episode"? An "extension"? Any other standard device?

Anything can be an extension, if, in such a classification, we are satisfied to include any insertion of a larger or smaller number of additional bars. Under such circumstances, the formative function of such additional bars can be utterly meaningless, and their classification under any heading can be as futile as an identical equation or an identical definition.

What elevates these two "extensions" of the Schubert Menuetto to the real function of creating, not *a* form, but FORM, is the fact that they, precisely they, are the very theater of the tension-relaxation duel, which we cannot escape feeling when we listen to the piece.

Here we see inspiration molded into sublimest form and, equally, form elevated to sublimest inspiration—the consummate absorption of each by the other.

Form versus number

It seems pertinent to remind ourselves again that proportions in artistic form, especially in musical form, do not coincide with arithmetical ones. We observe, on the contrary, that mathematical symmetry is rather apt to render form stiff and dead, and that, indeed, it is the barely perceptible irregularities which infuse life into artistic form. To be sure, it takes the subtlety and refinement of the accomplished artist to sense the appropriate places and quotas of the irregular.

In listening to the above Schubert Menuetto, one certainly gets the impression of the minutest equilibrium of form, both *in toto* and in detail. Yet the piece embraces a number of measures as odd as 55. Starting from the standard classical period of four or eight bars, one would arrive at this figure by such even greater oddities as 13 times 4 plus 3, or 7 times 8 minus 1. A closer investigation reveals that the deviations from the "regular" occur in precisely the two passages that cause so much delight: the first, through the timid, echo-like repetition of bar 26; the second, through the unexpected contraction of an expected four bar span into the startled hastiness, as it were, of the solitary bar 43.

A cursory glance at the bar numbers of Ex. 323 shows a far greater inequality of the sections, though it is no more conspicuous when the piece is actually played. The composition offers but one traditionally built eight-bar period, namely, the beginning of the march theme, bars 41-49. It is answered here by a 10 bar clause, while the answer of its restatement (188) loses itself in a high-arched climax, piling up disparate masses during a total of 15 bars. The first section of the piece (up to 27) consists, by a strange and amazing coincidence, of two *equal* subdivisions, each 13 bars long—their parity manifestly wholly accidental. And so it goes on, elevating irregularity to blessed law.

Though this persistency of the irregular is part of a highly personal style in the case of Wagner, classical literature is rife with similar, if more scattered, incommensurabilities.

The following example (325) may demonstrate how inspiration defies mathematical reasoning in the structure, not of a piece, but of a single theme.

325.

Mendelssohn, Violin-Concerto

Any attempt to restore mathematical symmetry in this theme must lead to the destruction of its wonderfully arched contour. There is no doubt that the three equal quarter-notes of bar 1 have the full weight of the arsis, as against the lesser weight of bar 2—thesis—of the metric construction. Yet gradually and imperceptibly this relation shifts. The three quarter-note figure, still in full arsis-character in bars 9, 11, 13, assumes more and more the up-beat tendency of the thesis, first in bar 17, more in 25, altogether in 35. The last instance, accentuating the downbeat of 36, makes bar 38 appear as though it were a contraction of two bars, with the entrance of the following theme coming in one bar too soon. Similarly, bar 25 blends thesis (after 24) and arsis (before 26) into one, thus anticipating the entrance of the theme by one bar. The part of the solo violin, drifting at this juncture in a lovely counterpoint to the theme, takes the lead soon again, mounting to a climax, unheedful of any considerations of structural symmetry.

CHAPTER XI

THE ART OF JOINING

The observation of such contractions as in the previous example, blending the end of an expiring phrase into the beginning of a new one, brings us closer to the subject of the "joints".

The ways of combining major or minor sections of a whole, the various transitions, retransitions, re-introductions, and the like, play an essential role in the matter of form. The joints are truly the spots where artistry meets artisanship, where genius meets technique, where the com-poser becomes the joiner.

As in oratory, drama and architecture, they are the spots of smooth transition, of unbroken flow, of linking preservation of movement. As in oratorical, dramatic or architectural structure, they are the spots to reveal taste, refinement and inventiveness in the hand of the skilful, or inept clumsiness in the hand of the unskilled.

Though the principle of overlapping and interlocking is common and basic to these joints, it works in manifold ways and takes on various appearances.

The method of telescoping a concluding section with a beginning, as suggested in bar 25 of Ex. 325, becomes clearly apparent in the following quotation (Ex. 326).

We would rather expect the transition to be as follows:

But the theme comes in sooner, carried pickaback, as it were, by the cadential bassoon passage of bars 20 and 21, and arriving in impatient anticipation at its second bar by the time the cadence is completed. The same device reoccurs at the beginning and at the end of the development of this movement. There, the transition, gliding down delicately on the motivic fabric and tapering gently off, slightly modifies the cadence:

The same method of planting the recapitulation midcourse of the subsiding cadence appears at the corresponding juncture in the first movement of Brahms' Second Symphony. The piece starts with a motive in the bass (Ex. 329, bar 1),

which appears unchanged in the bass of the little retransition before the repeat sign (Ex. 330, bar 8) :

In the final retransition, however, at the end of the development (Ex. 331), this first bar seems to have been lost:

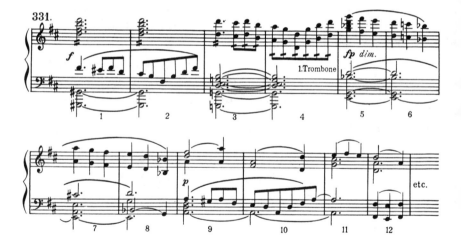

Yet, it is not. Utterly hidden in a seemingly insignificant middle voice, the first trombone (bars 5, 6, 7, 8), it is imbedded, telescoped into the structure of the flowing cadential harmonies, suggesting by the extended time values of its three notes the "written out ritardando".

What an enchanting, admirable subtlety!

Less concealed, yet equally delightful appears the same scheme in Ex. 330.

The end-and-beginning contraction of the joints appears sometimes reduced to the very instant of the contact. Ex. 332 shows a string of such "touch-and-go"s (marked by +) and their constructive, impelling effect.

332.

Brahms, Quartet Op. 51 No. 2

Examples 326 to 332 have in common the principle of advancing an approaching section (theme) to a point sooner than expected, thereby playing on the sensation of surprise. In examples 326 to 331 the entrance of the new section is wedged into the still progressing cadence, as diagrammed below (333a). In Ex. 332, the adjoining sections coincide tangentially (by way of deceptive cadences), as diagrammed in 333b.

a)

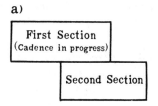

333.

b)

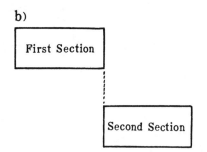

In the following we shall show methods of joining sections by a sort of *reversed* procedure. The psychological motive of surprise is now replaced by the one of preparedness. The oncoming section is properly invited, carefully announced, formally ushered in. The two sections are molded, almost welded together by the use of the second section's theme (or part of it) *before* its actual entrance, as a smooth and pleasant vehicle to lead into it.

Frequently, this is done by way of sequences, coming up from below, or down from above to the proper level of the so introduced theme.

334.

Mozart, Jupiter Symphony, Trio of the Menuetto

The above example (334) demonstrates this idea in the simplest form. Bars 17-22 consist of three sequences, each of them featuring one dominant-seventh chord and its natural

resolution. Measures 17-20 mediate between the preceding
and the following sections by retaining the rhythmical pulsation in an attenuated form, and dropping it altogether in
bar 21, thus disclosing the bare harmonies of the motif. Bars
21 and 22 act as the pivot between the abandonment of the
sequences and the entrance of the restatement.

In the following example, this pivot is represented by
bars 8 and 9 of the retransition. The passage, while showing
a highly artistic, contrapuntally rich tissue, is otherwise built
according to the same principle.

Even in fugal writing where unprepared entrances **of**
the theme prevail because of their enhanced plasticity, the in-
terludes sometimes usher in the theme by anticipatory sequences of its incipient motif (Ex. 336, 337, 338) .

An intermediate mode between pure sequences and pure

cadences is used in transitions like Ex. 339 and 340b.

While part of the roundness and pleasantness here rests in the fact that we are led smoothly *back* to a theme already familiar from previous parts of the respective compositions ("restatement"), we can be just as pleasantly led *forward* into a new theme, heard for the first time, a theme that

grows out of a motif pertaining to the transition itself. **Thus
for instance the "second theme" of a sonata may be fore-
shadowed:**

Mozart, Symphony .No. 38 (K. No. 504)

We do not know whether the composer preconceived his
second theme (Ex. 341) and tried to introduce it by retro-
spective adaptation, or whether the little flourish, adorning

in threefold repetition the preceding cadential chords, actually inspired and prompted the theme. Nor is such speculation any of our business. In any case, there it is, alive and
delightful; and in any case we get the indubitable impression
that the lovely theme *did* spring forth from the tiny, unpre-
tentious arabesque.

In a similar way the second theme of Beethoven's first
Piano Sonata (Ex. 342, bar 13) resumes the thread of the
preceding "bridge passage".

A closer examination of this bridge passage reveals that
it is organically linked to the contiguous sections *at both
ends.* For not only does it, at its own termination (bars 8-12),
foreshadow the new theme, but it evolves by spinning forth
the end of the preceding first theme (bar 2), using the little
motif in imitative style as a vehicle for the forthcoming
modulation (bars 3, 4, 5, 6).

Thus connecting links of any sort can originate by spinning forth the last musical idea, the last ramification of a terminating phrase.

It is natural that in such cases the beginning of the whole phrase (like bar 1 in Ex. 342) be dropped, and the molding be concentrated on the last motif (bars 3-6). Yet the same procedure of skipping the first motif and using only the second may also with advantage and added charm be applied to *introductory* links, like retransitions. Such a retransition, in contrast to examples 339-342, would not foreshadow the very beginning of the theme, but its immediate continuation, the second bar or so. We see this method applied to the retransition of the same Beethoven Sonata:

Here the motif is still more abridged than in the bridge passage of Ex. 342; in fact it is reduced almost to a grace-note figure. Skipping the first bar of the recapitulation (Ex. 343, bar 9), the little motif refers to the second bar (10). Note also how the pitch of the little figure in the theme itself (bar 10) is avoided before, so as to save its full effect for bar 10, while the upper line of the chain (bars 4, 6, 8) is gradually approaching this final pitch by stepwise descending sequences.

Similarly, in Ex. 344, it is the motive in the bass of the *second* bar of the theme (bar 6 of the example) that holds the lead among the motifs which, contrapuntally interwoven, make up the preceding retransition (bars 1, 2, 3, 4):

The following example presents an epitome of various ways of joining and molding together, as previously discussed.

345. Allegretto Grazioso

Brahms, Second Symphony

The movement starts with an eight bar phrase, ending on the dominant in the good old fashion. Even the suspension-resolution character of the two chords in bar 8 is familiar to us from innumerable encounters in classical music. Bar 9 repeats the formula, as if casually and haphazardly. Yet the idea of *spinning forth* the tiny motif of the upper voice gradually consolidates in bars 9-11, increasing each time the propelling power of the motif through changing harmonic interpretation. Now the vanishing spark of bar 8, gradually fanned through bars 9 and 10, flames up to new life. Bar 11 acts as the pivot between the old and the new. Bars 8-11 correspond to the bridge-passage of the Beethoven Sonata (Ex. 342, bar 1-12) in that here, too, the bridge is linked organically at both ends to the neighboring sections; except that here the integration is more concise and telling. The new theme thus introduced provides contrast by shifting tonality and emotional intensification up to bar 20. There the arch bends back again, using descending sequences (bars 21, 22) for a link to the restatement in bar 23. This bar is again the pivot on which two abutting sections hinge.

At another reprise, later in the piece, the telescoping device as shown in Ex. 326, 328, 330, 331, is used (Ex. 346).

346.

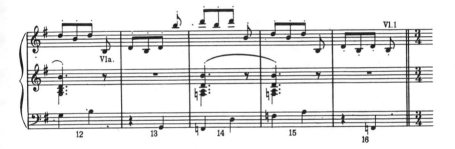

The process is still more telling here, in that the broad cadence, carrying the theme "pickaback" all the while, now almost fully coincides with the theme itself.

But the telescoping idea is much more firmly rooted here than by just the overlapping cadence as diagrammed in Ex. 333a. Harmony (the cadential progression) and melody (the dense motivic texture) combine to bind still closer the two adjacent sections.

The first section, approaching its end at this juncture, is marked by a motif in two-four time, appearing in the first ten bars of Ex. 346. The second section is marked by the main theme of the movement, starting in bar 17 at "Tempo primo". The intervening bars 11 through 16 represent the "joint".

The joint itself exhibits three layers. The uppermost, performed by violins and violas, continues the preceding section, bringing it to an end in bar 17. The middle layer, performed by woodwinds and horns, announces the on-coming main theme in a sparse and timid way, yet with sufficient distinctness. The motivic bridge is formed (1) by the sameness of the two upper pitches *b* and *d* of the wood-wind-chord; (2) by the sameness of instrumentation (the two oboes); (3) by shifting in bar 11 to a three-bar pattern which anticipates the triple meter of the ensuing theme; (4) by the *portamento* as indicated by the expression marks and the eighth rests at the end of bars 11, 12, 14, 15. All these means make the connection of this middle layer with the ensuing restatement (in which it becomes the upper layer) unmistakable. Just as unmistakable is, finally, the connection of the lowermost layer of the "joint"—the pizzicato figure in the cello—with the ensuing main part in which this instrumental group resumes its initial accompanying role in the smoothest and most natural manner, the changed notes now dictated by the harmonic requirements of the progressing cadence. If the highest note of this figure is omitted and replaced by a rest at the down-beats of bars 13 and 16, it is done so as to leave the register clear for the eighth-note motif in the strings (violas here) which at the same time link the two outermost layers in a fleeting contact.

Thus the smooth operation of the transition is three-foldly ensured. In the perfection of the *joint* we feel the skill of the *joiner,* tenoning and mortising, clinching and riveting the material of his creation. In *putting together* the proper parts in a proper way, he becomes the com - poser.

In the photoplay technique, adjoining scenes are connected either by "cuts" or by "dissolves". With a "cut" scenes follow each other sharply and without a transition. The "dissolve" uses an overlapping method, fading out one scene while the next simultaneously fades in, so that for a short while we see both pictures superimposed. Ex. 346 may be compared to such a dissolve. Bars 1 through 10 show the "picture" of the preceding section, approaching its end, but still "in the clear". In the clear, too, is the following section from bar 17 on, while bars 11 through 16 represent the "dissolve". In the same degree as the departing section (carried on by the upper layer of the violins and violas) fades out and loses significance, the arriving section of the lower layers fades in and gains significance. We notice that the composer indicated a *pp* for the upper string group, and at the same time a *p* for the part of the wind instruments (bar 11). The careful conductor will take this indication rather as a gradual *decrescendo* for the upper strings, to go along with a gradual, if light, *crescendo* for the wind group during the six bars of the dissolve (the latter followed by a *p dolce* again in bar 17).

Another surprising variant is provided in the next reprise (Ex. 347).

347.

The theme enters here in the key of F♯ major, carried there by a preceding modulation. Bars 8, 9, 10, 11 of Ex. 347 obviously correspond to the same bars of Ex. 345. But while there the upper part is retained with changing harmonies, here the harmonization is retained, with changing upper part. The melody in bar 11 continues sequentially, with abridged and shifted rhythmical pattern (indicated by ⌐‾‾⌐ ⌐‾‾⌐), the sequence smoothly gliding *in the middle of its course* to the familiar key and theme (bar 14).

CHAPTER XII

THE FORMATIVE INFLUENCE OF MOVEMENT

The various methods of joining tend to polish and smooth the edges of adjoining sections. They tend to conceal the gaping seams that obtain in primitive adherence to conventional formulas of structure. But most of all they make for unbroken flow, for continuous *movement,* and prevent faltering and stagnation.

Stagnation is the worst enemy of form; and since form and inspiration are so intimately interrelated, we may well say that stagnation is the worst enemy of inspiration. If inspiration dies, form is doomed to die with it. What keeps them alive, is essentially *movement.* Movement is far more than just a sign of life; indeed, it is *"the very essence of life"*.

It is a blessed wisdom of the English and French languages to call a complete division of a sonata or symphony a "movement". Thus in a terse way the product is identified with its most essential source. The Italian language also intimates the idea by calling such a section "Tempo".

But this continuous movement has little to do with inanely rolling sixteenths such as may be found in cheap "perpetuum mobile" compositions, full of empty sequences, or similar attempts at futile tone painting. Nor has the flow of a musical piece anything to do with speed. It applies to the slowest tempo as well as to the fastest.

As a model illustration of such unbroken flow I want to mention the Scherzo of Mendelssohn's "Midsummer Night's Dream" music—the most magnificent scherzo of our literature, not excepting Beethoven. So incessant is the torrent of this music that the composer just could not afford to interrupt it by inserting the obligatory "Trio". A composer knowing *the forms* would have added it. Its composer, knowing FORM, had to omit it.

Manifold are the means of keeping a composition in flow.

Take Prelude VI, in *d* minor, from the first volume of Bach's "Well-tempered Clavichord". The sweeping vitality of the piece, its unbroken flow, is brought about by the maintenance of a tiny triplet motif which pervades the entire piece, filling its arteries, as it were, with a homogeneous blood-substance.

Now take the first movement of Bach's "Italian Concerto". Here, too, there certainly is no danger of stagnation, as ever with Bach. But as to the propelling motor that keeps the movement moving, the piece appears somehow diametrically contrasting to the previously quoted *d* minor Prelude. For here, apart from the concluding section which rounds off the form, and apart from occasional motivic references, we see the thematic material constantly renewing itself in abounding richness, as if drawn from an inexhaustible cornucopia. Technical device is almost completely superseded by sheer inspiration — in truth, the best device of all!

The two pieces, reaching the common goal—unbroken flow—by opposite means, stand for innumerable other examples of their respective types. With regard to the maintenance of movement by motivic treatment, they represent the two extremes between which this kind of treatment varies —perpetuation of one motif, and accumulation of various motifs.

At any rate, the chief pervading principle is again: Avoid the worst enemy of form — stagnation!

Stagnation means the slackening or even breaking of the thread of musical narration.

If the concert-hall audience bursts into premature applause, taking a pronounced full cadence for the end of the piece, it is never their fault; rather is it wholly and solely the fault of the composer, and only he, not the audience, should feel embarrassed and punished. That will occasionally happen even with the greatest masters of the classical period, who sometimes were trapped in the routine of certain formal prototypes of which the average listener is innocent and ignorant. It will, however, not happen with Bach, who fortunately lived and created before formalism of stereotyped structure could congeal, and who therefore was able to follow his superior form-instinct, unhampered by the hazards of ingrained sonata-routine. Nor will it happen with Brahms, whose refined taste and subtlety, in revision of his predecessors' habits, rejected the conspicuously exposed seams of the conventional structure.

Another source of the stagnation danger lies in the opposite direction. It concerns the attenuation of the thread of narration by drawing it out excessively.

Conciseness makes for flow, protraction is apt to reduce flow to a trickle.

Mere cuts may help sometimes; but in other instances, especially with compositions of a finer and more intricate texture, mere cuts will not do, but must be supplemented by skilfully repairing the texture. (The effect of contraction on unbroken flow with respect to the *joints* was touched upon in Ex. 326-347).

The stagnating effect of protraction is often reducible to repetitiousness.

There is a peculiar thing about repetition in music. Music by and large is almost inconceivable without repetition. It is the rhythmical recurrence of a motivic pattern that provides the unifying undercurrent of sections, at least, if not of whole movements. Besides, we welcome the recurrence of themes as another means of unification and formal support to musical structure. And yet we are apt to take for mere repetition what the master, in pursuit of continuous flow, may present in constantly changing appearance, giving us just enough of the repetition to enjoy the acquaintance, and at the same time just enough of variation to enjoy subconsciously the constant renewal.

How many musicians or music lovers, who have heard, played or conducted Mozart's popular G Minor Symphony uncounted times and believe they know "every bar of it", would volunteer to reproduce extempore the second theme of its last movement?

There is nothing particularly tricky about this theme; on the contrary, we recollect it as a simple theme, built in regular period structure.

An eight bar phrase evidently recurs four times in the statement, and as many times, transposed into the original key of *g* minor, in the restatement.

Here are the eight "repetitions":

348 a)

Mozart, Symphony K. No. 550

348 b)

ibidem

Which is "the theme"? Each of the eight phrases could be it, and each a variant of each. Apparently alike for the listener, they are all different, considerably and delightfully different, even to the linking bars of the transitions. With such an unlimited supply of new ideas no stagnation can arise.

Motif and theme

If we compare bars 7 and 23 of Ex. 348b, we see that the bass of 23 slightly varies the bass of bar 7, in that it replaces the mere repetition of the *d* by alternating it with its neighbor tone, *c♯*. The same little bass figure appears also in the corresponding bar 23 of 348a; but while it has no further consequences there, here it is picked up and imitated in the following bars. Yet such imitations, commonplace in the province of counterpoint, become ever so much more than a contrapuntal sport in the domain of FORM. They keep movement rolling by the alternate emergence and submergence of the motif. The little motif of bar 23 (Ex. 348b), submerged here, emerges in bar 24, at the same time serving as an introduction to the theme. Submerging in bars 25 and 26, it emerges again in bars 27 and 28 as a new, varied continuation of the theme, during which, in turn, the beginning of the theme submerges into the tenor voice of bars 27 and 28. Thus counterpoint becomes *functional*. It assumes a real and quite essential formative function in that it exercises a *propelling force*.

No motif is too small, too insignificant, too negligible to promote, not only construction and movement, but inspiration itself, as is apparent in this last phrase. No motif is insignificant enough to be discarded for that reason.

Every combination of a few tones is apt to become a

motif and, as such, to pervade and feed the cellular tissue of a composition, emerging and submerging alternately, giving and receiving support and significance by turns. It revives and animates, and is revived and animated, in a continuous cycle of give and take. It lives on repetition and yet on constant metamorphosis; metamorphic, polymorphic, opalescent in itself, it takes on the hue, the flavor, the very mood of the environment in which it is imbedded. It smoothes and ruffles, it soothes and arouses; it bridges and reconciles, glues and splices, planes and levels, polishes and varnishes. But above all, it creates and feeds movement, movement, movement, *the very essence of life,* and fends off the arch-enemy, stagnation, the very essence of death.

It, the little motif, becomes the motive, the motive power, the MOTOR.

In Ex. 349 the theme starts with a weightless, introductory figure in the bass (bar 1). We have already dealt with this figure in another connection (Ex. 329-331). Now let us examine the first main section of this movement, including the first theme and transition passage, up to the second theme (Ex. 349).

349. Allegro ma non troppo   Brahms, Sec. Symphony Op.73, first mvt.

In listening to the beginning of this movement, our main attention is taken up by the serene and noble lines in horns and woodwinds (bars 2 to 20) which make the little introductory motif of the string basses (bar 1) appear still more insignificant. It gradually gains weight by repetition (bars 5, 9, 13) until its functional part in the organism is established, though the listener—absorbed by the events of the upper voices, the real "theme"—is still hardly conscious of its existence.

In bars 35 and 39 the motif emerges from its subdued role, loftily exposed now to our attention; and it is now that we consciously or half-consciously begin to link it with the first bar of the piece, as its tender reverberation.

Its augmented appearance in bars 42 and 43 makes the effect of a written out ritardando, thus announcing the advent of something new. This something new—the "transition section"—indeed starts in bar 44.

But how? Again it is the same three tones of the motif that connect the two sections. Yet, having been held back by the augmented time-values, the motif (showing rhythmical elasticity as discussed on page 98ff) now releases a row of quick, resilient tones which create a more lively and animated mood.

The motif has entered its first metamorphosis.

The animation is increased by a fourfold stretto, the

motif chasing itself through bars 52, 53, 54, 55. The momentum so gained leads to a temporary climax (59) in which the motif, in lieu of the displaced theme, obtains complete, if temporary, sovereignty. Appearing now in different registers (59, 61, 63), it performs the modulation pertinent to the transition section. Bars 64 and 65 reveal it splitting the bar in two halves by its own reduction to half time. Here it undergoes its second metamorphosis which is quickly to be followed by another one in bar 66. Though the actual tones of the upper voice in this bar (66) do not differ from the two preceding bars, it is most of all the woodwind staccato, as against the preceding string legato, that brings about a complete change in mood. The motif has now taken on a pronounced *scherzando* character. If compared with its first occurrence in bar 1, it appears now almost unrecognizably disguised.

At the same time, however, it is in a way more closely connected with its original form than in the completely undisguised versions in bars 35, 39, 42-43. There it comprises actually the three notes of the first bar. From bar 59 on, however, it also embraces the following bar, as expressed by the leap of a fourth, up or down, according to the tonic-dominant relation. Thus measures 59-60 correspond to 1-2, as do 61-62 and 63-64. From 66 on measures 9-10, or 13-14, serve as a model. The added tone, the fourth tone of the figure, becomes more and more essential in that it changes the silhouette of the motif. In bar 71 and thereafter, the outer frame of this silhouette is all that is left of it. With these last remnants it tapers off, completely fading out in bar 78.

So it is not the first theme, but the little introductory motif that actually feeds the whole section from its rise in the first bar to its expiration at the threshold of the second theme.

Needless to say, its play is resumed and still more rami-
fied in the development section up to its submersion as
shown in Ex. 331, and again in the recapitulation and coda.
There it lingers, interwoven with other motifs, and finally
speaks the last word of the dying movement, as it spoke the
first, in the beginning (Ex. 350).:

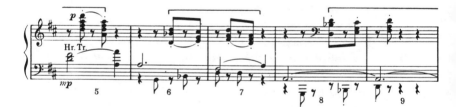

Again the motif appears in both the three-tone (bars 1-3) and the four-tone (6-10) form; besides, it appears in stretto (1-3), as introduced in the (here omitted) development section. In its longer form (6-10), its relation to the beats is shifted, providing another change which makes itself palpably felt and avoids mere repetition. In these bars (6-10) it circumplays the last echoing reminiscences of the main theme, which is also reduced here, like a dying spark, to the fragmentary size of a motif.

Still, we are much more conscious of the theme, in spite of its fragmentary size, than of the circumplaying motif. And we are more conscious of the theme in spite of its scattered and intermittent presences than we are of the omnipresent, flowing, rolling motif.

For the theme announces and asserts its presence (compare the entrance of the second theme in bar 82, Ex. 349); the motif sneaks in and sneaks out, and meanwhile travels and meanders, unobtrusively and under the surface, as it were.

The theme is sizable, clearly shaped and clean cut; it has its countenance, its character, its mood. The motif is loose jointed, limber, flexible and versatile; it plays in a thousand colors and assimilates a thousand moods.

The theme strides and poses, stamping its seal on our mind, while underneath the nimble motif glides and flits and all but escapes our attention.

The theme cannot force its weight through the delicate veins and ramifications of the cellular texture, which the swift and fluid motif easily penetrates.

Look at a building. You cannot overlook the doors, windows and balconies, all in proper place and position.

But of little avail would be their proper place and position, were it not for the *building material*—the handy, adaptable bricks that fill the space between them, surrounding, supporting, cementing them, keeping them properly together and properly apart.

In Ex. 349 we viewed a section of such a façade, made up mostly of the building material between the first theme and the second, of which we indicated only the first bar (82). We pursued the motif through its various metamorphoses from its origin to its expiration. Could we have missed anything? Let us see.

When the motif is brought to full focus in bar 59, we see it accompanied by what appears to be a broken harmony in a lower voice. Nothing in particular seems to distinguish this harmonic support of the motif, except that the breaking of the chord reveals a certain pattern. This pattern repeats in bar 61, with the registers of the voices interchanged, and again in bar 63 with registers restored. By now we feel that the pattern of the broken harmony, meant to be an accompaniment at first, is on the way to establishing itself motivically. This feeling grows with bars 66-67 when the two motifs, bound together at first, begin to separate from one another. This separation asserts itself in the two following sequences (bars 68-71), at the same time emphasizing the independence of the two motifs. With bar 71, the first motif is reduced to the extremes of its silhouette, leaving the field —and the task of propulsion— to the second motif. The few remaining bars (up to 78) show the first motif submerging in the same degree as the second motif simultaneously emerges, approaching again the "dissolve" technique of Ex. 346. When the second theme, after a few bars of transition,

starts (82), the first motif is definitely dropped and replaced by the second motif, which accompanies the second
theme for a while and, later on, gets lost in the course of the
following events.

Epitomizing this brief analysis: The pillars of this section as viewed so far are the two themes. The space between
them is occupied by building material. This building material is not sawdust and stuffing, but *live, organic fibre*. It is
made up of two motifs, independent of one another and of
the two themes, though the first motif is closely attached to
the first theme and the second motif is loosely attached to
the second theme. These two motifs relieve each other in
the course of the building process. However, this relief is
brought about not by juxtaposition but by overlapping and
gradual dissolve.

We are fully conscious of the themes whose distinguish-
ing mark is prominence and impressiveness, and whose function, architecturally and psychologically, is to act as the
salient landmarks of the composition.

We are only partly conscious of the motifs, whose mark
is *un*prominence and restraint, and whose invaluable function is to build, to cement, to keep life alive, to continue, to
promote and propel — all this in the service of that supreme
artistic demand, which is at the same time supreme artistic
benefactor: F O R M .

The thematic motif

As an aerolite may break from a heavenly body and
continue gyrating for a while by its own power, so may a
particle of the solid theme break away and, in motif manner,
circle around its generator (Ex. 351).

It is not the contrapuntal device that constitutes the virtue of the "imitation" in bar 2 and later in bar 4 but its formative function, easily to be seen in the ensuing bars.

Activated by the last offshoot of the phrase, the figure, now a motif in itself, reactivates its source (bar 5, 1st vl.,) and persists in the cello, while the leading voice sings out its lyrical sequel. Splitting in half now, aerolite fashion again, the motif appears to taper off (10) ; yet, the split fragment rekindles the other voices (12) and they reflect the fragment, its tonal pattern imperceptibly changed now, in playful imitations. Again it flares up and in a last rise brings the passage to an end.

Again, the motif is as small and insignificant as can be. That is why it hardly enters our consciousness; yet, when listening to the melody of the leading voice in bars 6-11, we pleasantly, if unconsciously, feel its simultaneous generating function. This function is enhanced by the polyphonic, or semi-polyphonic setting.

Beethoven was not particularly polyphony-minded. His mind worked in other directions. Yet he, too, knew, or knew without knowing that he knew, the constructive value of the smallest, the most insignificant particle of a theme.

For that matter, what else should such a particle be but insignificant? Suppose you are admiring the exquisitely curved lines of a drawing. If you divide such a line into tiny particles, will not these fragments necessarily lose their prominence and grandeur? By the same token the most wonderful poem is composed of words which, individually, show no trace of uniqueness, but are bound to be used over and over again by the most prosaic mind in the most prosaic connection.

The first theme of Beethoven's Pastoral Symphony consists of four two-four bars (Ex. 352).

Short as this theme is, it contains enough material to feed no less than two thirds (to be exact, 337 out of 512 bars) of the movement. This material consists of a number of motifs, each equivalent to a bar, or even a half bar, of the theme. In contrast to Ex. 349, the diversities of the motifs here are not of rhythmical but of tonal nature, while the rhythm, the more essential motivic element, is retained. The composition shows that *nothing is wasted;* that nothing is too small to form a cell of the structure and to maintain the smooth, undulating flow.

Due to the almost completely homophonic style of the composition, the motifs do not form an undercurrent here, but always constitute the leading voice, though sometimes in lower registers. Thus they can easily be exhibited detached, in one voice (Ex. 353-367).

352.   (theme)

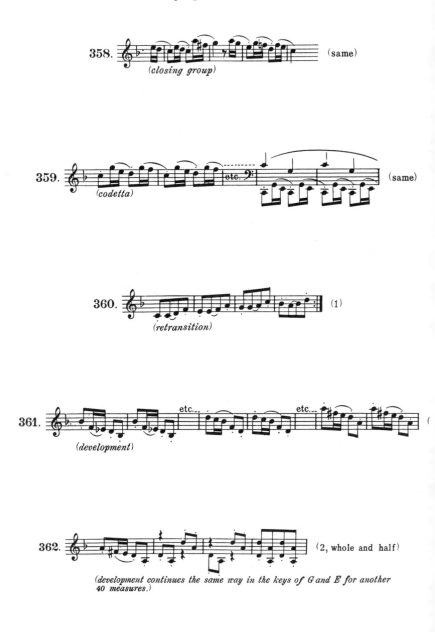

363. (2)

(2)

(Still development.) Follows recapitulation unfolding all the material again.

365. *(Coda)* (half of 2 or 3)

Only in two places, the motifs show a rhythmical variation to triplets: (Ex. 366, 367)

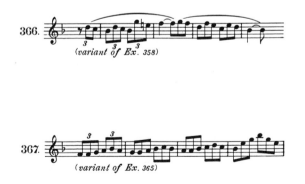

366. *(variant of Ex. 358)*

367. *(variant of Ex. 365)*

The confinement of the motif material to the leading voice, and the resulting absence of a fine-spun, motivically interwoven texture, make this kind of composition appear simple almost to the point of primitivity, if contrasted to the subtle artistry of Mozart or Brahms.

Does that mean fault or virtue? It certainly means both. One thing, however, is certain: If you want to study the *craft,* you had better enroll with Mozart.

CHAPTER XIII

BEGINNING AND ENDING

Having dealt so far mainly with the items conducive to the structure and fluency of music *in progress,* let us now look into the beginning and ending of a composition.

As a narrative may start either by plunging *medias in res,* or by first creating an introductory general atmosphere of location, time, situation, etc., or by a completely detached introduction, prologue or preface; so may a musical narrative show different types of beginnings, roughly corresponding to those mentioned above.

Ex. 368-72 illustrate the "plunging *medias in res*" type.

R. Strauss, "Don Juan"

369.

R. Strauss,"Rosenkavalier"

370.

R. Strauss, "Salome"

371.

372.

In the prime of our classical music, composers liked to start a larger, especially a symphonic, piece with an introduction in slow tempo. This introduction usually was a completely detached statement, grave and austere in mood. sometimes also leading into the main part by direct motivic preparation (Ex. 373).

Sometimes it would assume the character of a vague improvisation, starting from afar (Ex. 374), or would start like a brewing mist, gradually dissipating and giving way to the bright light, as in Mozart's famous "Dissonant" Quartet (Ex. 375).

373.

374. Adagio

Beethoven, Overture No. 3, Leonore

375.
Adagio

Mozart, Quartet K. No. 465

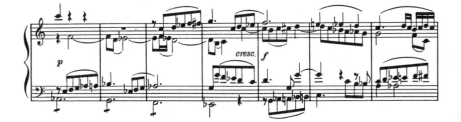

Beethoven started his first two symphonies with slow introductions, pretty much in the traditional style. To the revolutionary spirit and attitude of the third symphony, however, such an introduction would not fit. It would perhaps minimize this spirit rather than promote it. On the other hand, to put the first theme bluntly and nakedly at the beginning, would be equally unsatisfactory; for the theme, with all its greatness, lacks the dramatic bite of the *medias in res* type. Again Beethoven cut the Gordian knot by resorting to utter primitivity, and again this primitivity proved a blessed inspiration. The traditional "introduction" is reduced to two mere flashes of the tonic triad which open the wild chase of the movement (Ex. 376).

376.

Allegro con brio

Beethoven, Third Symphony

The starting "from afar", as shown in Ex. 374, is not
limited to the improvisational, detached introduction of a
piece, but may just as well open the main theme itself
(Ex. 377).

This way of beginning creates a certain suspense and
gives the opening, as it were, an obliquity which has to be
straightened. The straightening is achieved when the tonic
harmony is reached (Ex. 377, bar 6 and still more bar 8).
In this moment, the suspense ceases and gives way to the
feeling of assertion.

This type of opening has a particularly romantic character. No piece of Bach, or of his epoch, is known to me
that would start otherwise than with the tonic triad, or, if
in a single voice, with the tonic harmony suggested.

The suspense of the harmonic obliquity can be protracted considerably.

In Schumann's song "Mondnacht" (Ex. 378) the tonic
triad, to be sure, occurs in bar 10; yet, accentless and subdued
to the role of ushering in the powerful dominant half
cadence (bar 13), it has no weight, no import of its own.
It is not before bar 59 that the singing voice, at least, reaches
its "home" (text: "als flöge sie *nach Haus*"—"as though it
would fly *home*"). The full tonic effect, however, is still
evaded by the deflection of the bass and the deceptive har-

monization of the accompaniment. Only two bars later, at the downbeat of bar 61, the long yearned for assertion and repose comes to pass, in the nick of time, when the whole song is practically over.

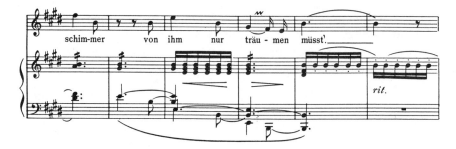

schim-mer   von ihm   nur träu - men müsst'.

rit.

rit.

Die   Luft   ging   durch die Fel-der,   die

Äh - ren   wog - ten sacht,   es rausch-ten

leis' die Wäl - der, so stern - klar war die

Nacht. Und mei - ne See - le

spann - te weit ih - re Flü - gel

aus, flog durch die stil - len Lan - de,

It must be hoped that the reader feels the tremendous influence of this manner of expression on the FORM of the composition, the manner of expression being the distant beginning and long delayed arrival, and FORM the material realization of the spiritual image — another definition of FORM, if you like.

The most amazing example of this type presents itself in Schumann's "Fantasy", op. 17, first movement. The tripartite piece starts with oblique harmony and reaches the end of its first section (bar 128) without ever arriving at the tonic triad. It continues its restless travels through constantly changing keys, moods, material, with no reference anywhere to the main key. No sooner than in bar 308—13 bars before the end of the piece—the "arrival" announces itself, spreading throughout these last 13 bars, the final repose still delayed by ever so pungent retardations up to the very end. The wide-stretched arch of the piece may be likened to Lindbergh's nonstop flight from New York to Paris in 1927, or to the high-arched curve of a star shooting through the whole celestial vault.

The ending of a musical piece, too, may show traits similar to those just discussed for the beginning.

If we spoke of a *medias in res* type, as shown in Ex. 368-372, we understood by that a beginning that would plunge into the narration point blank, without any ado. To this kind of a beginning would correspond a kind of ending also point blank, without any ado, the narration carried up to the last word, or bar, or sound; and after that no word wasted. If there were such a term as "mediis ex rebus", it would be the corresponding term.

Here are a few examples of this type (379-385):

380.

381.

382.

In most instances (Ex. 379, 380, 383-385) the thematic
material is used up to the last bar or sound. In some instances, the theme is just in time to catch up with the last
chord (Ex. 379, 380, 384, 385). In other instances, the theme,
or motif, is even late, and its extreme tip still protrudes beyond the concluding chord (Ex. 381, 382). With these end-

ings, a composition brims over with real substance; so much
so that out of the very closing phrase its subject, or theme,
could be reconstructed.

It would certainly be difficult to reconstruct any
thematic substance out of a "closing phrase" like the following, which may illustrate the preceding idea by contrast
(Ex. 386):

The reader may object: Though certainly a contrast, why must it be laid on so thick, artificially and superfluously?

With grief it must be stated that this example is not made up fictitiously. It is a literal quotation, a quotation, in fact, from the most popular of the classical symphonies. Here primitivity, a blessing in so many other instances, turns into a perfect nightmare. To be sure, these 41 last bars of Beethoven's Fifth Symphony are led up to by other preceding bars. Yet no other brain would have contrived this peculiar chariot to carry a conductor (any conductor) to the triumph of a glory-bedecked hero. It leads one to believe the current story of one such conductor who, jerked around prematurely by the frenzied cheers of a hypnotized audience that just could not restrain its ecstasy any longer, quickly bowed to the raging masses and, wheeling back again was just in time to deal, a victorious gladiator, the deadly finishing stroke.

If Ex. 379-382 represent an accelerating type of conclusion, Ex. 386 shows the antipode of this type, namely the
retarding, broadening type of conclusion, in its most primitive form, brought about by the hypnotic effect of excessive
repetition. Other and nobler illustrations of the retarding
conclusion are shown in Ex. 387-390.

387. Adagissimo   Bach, Organ-Toccata D minor

388.

Adagio

Bach, W. Cl. I, Prelude 2

389.

Bach, W. Cl. I, Fugue 1

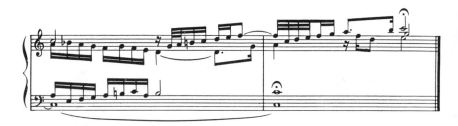

390.

Bach, W. Cl. I, Prelude 8

The endings in these examples, as compared with **Ex.** 379-382, are no longer precipitous. They do not assert themselves by pounding the tonic profusely; on the contrary, the relieving final harmony of the tonic appears now reserved for the very last sound. Before that, the harmonies grope their way in spreading ramifications like those of a huge river delta. As the waters of the delta, struggling along in the last phase of their journey, follow the irresistible call of Mother Ocean, so these harmonies, straying in desperate agony of search, call for acceptance and are called into acceptance by Mother Tonic.

This effect is particularly stressed if the tonic is planted in the bass long before the close and is sustained there up to the end as a "pedal point". It attracts the other voices like a magnet until it embraces and absorbs them in the tonic triad. (Ex. 388-390). This final triad makes the effect of inexorable consummation of Destiny, and at the same time of the longed for peace and consolation.

The following poem by Goethe may perhaps serve as a linguistic analogy.

Wanderers Nachtlied

Der du von dem Himmel bist,
Alles Leid und Schmerzen stillest,
Den, der doppelt elend ist,
Doppelt mit Erquickung füllest,
Ach, ich bin des Treibens müde!
Was soll all der Schmerz und Lust?
Süsser Friede,
Komm, ach komm in meine Brust!

The Wanderer's Night Song

Thou who comest from on high,
Who all woes and sorrows stillest,
Who, for twofold misery,
Hearts with twofold balsam fillest,
Would this constant strife would cease!
What are pain and rapture now?
Blissful peace,
To my bosom hasten thou!

(*English version by E. A. Bowring*)

Does not the "Thou" of the first line which sustains the "keynote" up to the last line, resemble the pedal point of the tonic? Does not the parenthesis of lines 5 and 6 in its complete detachment correspond to the harmonically detached "straying" voices over the pedal point? And the last two lines, consummating the invocation of the preposed "Thou", to the final triad which also consummates the call of the preposed keynote? And even spiritually, does not the final triad (especially in Ex. 390) likewise suggest the appeal to the great Comforter, Peace?

What has been said and shown here on the subject of form, is by no means meant to be a comprehensive theory. In fact it is a tiny, perhaps an infinitesimal part of it.

Though the examples for demonstration have been chiefly chosen from the classical literature, as part of the general musical consciousness, more accessible and traceable for that reason, the *formative principles* shown at work are not bound to any particular style or epoch or idiom. Even where tonality and key have a bearing, for instance in the relation of tension and attraction between secondary steps and tonic, it is the unchangeable *effect* which is aimed at, not the changeable and constantly changing *means*.

Sometimes we may have made a statement the opposite of which may be equally true. This fact does not render the knowledge and application of *either one* less useful and desirable. If all paths lead to Rome, it is still good to know them all and remain the master of one's own choice. If the proverb is taken literally, the consideration of all circumstances involved may lead to an "opposite" choice, or any one in between. The same holds good if the proverb is taken figuratively. One should know the ways in order to be able to try them out and arrive at an ultimate choice. It remains largely unknown how many sketches the master may have rejected before arriving at the expression that seems so natural and unquestionable to the naive listener.

In any narrative—epic, dramatic or musical—every word or tone should be like a soldier marching towards the one, common, final goal: *conquest of the material*. The way the artist makes every phrase of his story such a soldier, serving to unfold it, to support its structure and development, to build plot and counterplot, to distribute light and shade, to point incessantly and lead up gradually to the climax, in short the way every fragment is impregnated with its mission towards the whole, makes up this delicate and so essential objective which we call F O R M.

CHECKLIST OF COMPOSITIONS
BY ERNST TOCH

The following pages constitute a newly revised listing, as complete as possible, of Ernst Toch's music, with indications of published works currently available (1976), lost works and works that can be examined in manuscript or other form in the Ernst Toch Archive.

The publishers represented are:

B. Schott's Söhne, Mainz, West Germany (abbreviated here as "Schott"; American representative: Belwin-Mills).

Belwin-Mills Publishing Corporation, New York and Berlin.

Associated Music Publishers, a division of G. Schirmer, Inc., New York (European representative: Bote & Bock, Berlin).

MCA Music (Leeds), New York.

The Ernst Toch Archive is housed in the Music Library of the University of California, Los Angeles. A center of research for Toch studies, the Archive includes manuscripts, papers, recordings and a complete collection of both published and unpublished music.

In compiling the present checklist, much use has been made of the definitive chronological list and thematic catalogue of Toch's works included in Charles Johnson's 1973 Ph.D. dissertation for the University of California, Los Angeles, *The Unpublished Music of Ernst Toch*. For the film music, Clifford McCarty's book *Film Composers in America* (Da Capo, New York, 1972) has been consulted.

CONTENTS

Operas

Die Prinzessin auf der Erbse [The Princess and the Pea], Op. 43 (1927)
Musical fairy tale in one act; text after H. C. Andersen by Benno Elkan.
Pub. by Schott (separate German and English vocal scores).
* The overture is pub. separately by Schott as *Vorspiel zu einem Märchen*
[Overture to a Fairy Tale].

Egon und Emilie [Edgar and Emily], Op. 46 (1928)
"Not a family drama" (*Kein Familiendrama*); text by Christian Morgen-
stern.
Pub. by Schott (separate German and English vocal scores).

Der Fächer [The Fan], Op. 51 (1930)
Opera-capriccio in three acts; text by Ferdinand Lion.
Pub. by Schott.
* The overture is also pub. separately.

The Last Tale, Op. 88 (1962) [a Sheherazade opera]
Opera in one act; text by Melchior Lengyel, English translation by Cor-
nel Lengyel.
Pub. by Belwin-Mills (combined English and German vocal score).

Orchestral Works

Scherzo, Op. 11 (1904)
Archive.

Kammersymphonie F-Dur [Chamber Symphony in F Major] (1906)
For 10 instruments; in one movement; motto: "Immer strebe zum Gan-

zen" (Always strive for the whole); Mozart Prize winner.
Archive.

Phantastische Nachtmusik [Fantastic Serenade], Op. 27 (1920)
Archive.

Fünf Stücke für Kammerorchester [Five Pieces for Chamber Orchestra],
Op. 33 (1924)
1. Langsam [Slow]. 2. Ruhig [Calm]. 3. Intermezzo. 4. Heftig, eigenwillig
[Violent, willful]. 5. Allegro assai.
Pub. by Schott.

Narziss [Narcissus] (1927?)
Ballet.
Lost.

Gewitter [Storm] (1927?)
Ballet.
Lost.

Komödie für Orchester in einem Satz [Comedy for Orchestra in One
Movement], Op. 42 (1927)
Pub. by Schott.

Vorspiel zu einem Märchen: *see* Die Prinzessin auf der Erbse (page 240)

Bunte Suite [Motley Suite], Op. 48 (1928)
1. Marschtempo [March Tempo]. 2. Intermezzo. 3. Adagio espressivo.
4. Marionetten-Tanz [Marionette Dance]. 5. Galante Passacaglia [Amor-
ous Passacaglia]. 6. Karussell (Carousel).
Pub. by Schott.

Der Fächer; Kleine Ouvertüre zu der Oper: *see* Der Fächer (page 240)

Kleine Theater-Suite [Little Theater Suite], Op. 54 (1931)
1. Ouvertüre. 2. Schüchterne Werbung [Shy Wooing]. 3. Tanz [Dance].
4. Nachtstück [Nocturne]. 5. Finale.
Pub. by Schott.

Tragische Musik (1931?)
Lost.

Big Ben; Variationen über das Westminster-Geläut [Variation Fantasy
on the Westminster Chimes], Op. 62 (1935)
Pub. by Associated Music Publishers.

Pinocchio; A Merry Overture (1935)
Pub. by Associated Music Publishers.

Musical Short Story (1936)
Lost.

Orchids Suite (1936)
Lost.

"The Idle Stroller" Suite (1938)
1. Starting Off. 2. Gossamer. 3. Distant Memories. 4. Striding Onward.
5. Lingering Thoughts. 6. Joyous Return.
Archive.

The Covenant (1945)
A phonograph recording exists but the score is lost; this was one movement of the six-movement *Genesis Suite* conceived by Nathaniel Shilkret of the Victor Recording Co.; the other composers involved were Schoenberg, Stravinsky, Milhaud, Castelnuovo-Tedesco and Shilkret himself.
Archive.

Hyperion; A Dramatic Prelude for Orchestra, Op. 71 (1947)
Study score pub. by MCA Music (Leeds).

Dedication (1948)
For string quartet or string orchestra; a short wedding march.
Pub. by Belwin-Mills.

Symphony No. 1, Op. 72 (1949/50)
For large orchestra.
1. Molto tranquillo. 2. Allegro molto. 3. Adagio. 4. Allegro non troppo.
Study score pub. by Schott.

Symphony No. 2, Op. 73 (1953)
Dedicated to Albert Schweitzer.
1. Allegro fanatico. 2. Scherzo. 3. Adagio. 4. Allegro.
Study score pub. by Associated Music Publishers.

Notturno, Op. 77 (1953)
Commissioned by the Louisville Symphony Orchestra.
Study score pub. by Belwin-Mills.

Prelude and Fugue for String Orchestra (1953)
Freely transcribed from J. S. Bach's Solo Violin Sonata No. 3 in C Major.
Pub. by Belwin-Mills.

Circus Overture (1954)
Pub. by Belwin-Mills.

Symphony No. 3, Op. 75 (1954/55)
Commissioned by the American Jewish Tercentenary Committee of Chicago; Pulitzer Prize 1956.
1. Molto adagio – Agitato – Tempo primo. 2. Andante tranquillo. 3. Al-

legro impetuoso.
Study score pub. by Belwin-Mills.

Peter Pan; Fairy Tale for Orchestra in Three Parts, Op. 76 (1956)
Commissioned by the Koussevitsky Foundation.
1. Allegro giocoso. 2. Allegretto grazioso. 3. Allegro vivo.
Study score pub. by Schott.

Symphony No. 4, Op. 80 (1957)
Commissioned by the Woman's Association of the Minneapolis Symphony Orchestra. Dedicated to Miriam MacDowell.
1. Molto dolce – Molto tranquillo – Molto egualmente. 2. Lively (Con brio). 3. Molto grave.
Study score pub. by Belwin-Mills.

Three Pieces for Doctor's Orchestra, Op. 82
1. Short Story (1960). 2. Intermezzo (1960). 3. Epilogue (1961).
Pub. by Belwin-Mills.

Jephta; Rhapsodic Poem (= Symphony No. 5), Op. 89 (1961/62)
Dedicated to Lion Feuchtwanger.
In one movement.
Study score pub. by Belwin-Mills.

Three Pantomimes for Orchestra (1963/64)
1. Puppet Show, Op. 92
2. Capriccio, Op. 91
3. The Enamoured Harlequin, Op. 94
Pub. by Belwin-Mills.

Symphony No. 6, Op. 93 (1963)
1. Allegro comodo. 2. Molto grazioso e leggiero. 3. Allegro energico.
Study score pub. by Belwin-Mills.

Symphony No. 7, Op. 95 (1964)
1. Molto lento – Allegro moderato. 2. Allegro giocoso. 3. Allegro risoluto.
Study score pub. by Belwin-Mills.

Sinfonietta for String Orchestra, Op. 96 (1964)
1. Allegro moderato. 2. Andante cantabile. 3. Allegro giocoso.
Study score pub. by Belwin-Mills.

Variations on the Swabian Folk Song "Muss i denn zum Städle hinaus,"
op. post.
Pub. by Belwin-Mills.

Works for Wind Orchestra

Spiel für Blasorchester [Divertimento for Wind Orchestra], Op. 39 (1926)
1. Ouvertüre. 2. Idyll. 3. Buffo.
Pub. by Schott.

Klangfilm Ouvertüre [Sound Film Overture] (c. 1929)
May be the same as *Miniatur Ouvertüre*; otherwise, lost.

Zwei kultische Stücke [Two Cultic Pieces] (1932)
Lost.

Miniatur Ouvertüre (1932)
Pub. by Ars Viva (Schott).

Sinfonietta for Wind Orchestra, Op. 97 (1964)
1. (No tempo indication). 2. Andante flebile; "Life Without a Dog." 3.
(No tempo indication) "Thank Goodness He Barks Again."
Study score pub. by Belwin-Mills.

Works for Solo Instruments and Orchestra

Concerto for Piano and Orchestra in A Major (1904)
Lost.

Concerto for Violoncello and Chamber Orchestra, Op. 35 (1925)
1. Allegro assai moderato. 2. Agitato. 3. Adagio. 4. Allegro vivace.
Cello-piano version and study score pub. by Schott.

Concerto for Piano and Orchestra (No. 1), Op. 38 (1926)
1. Molto pesante. 2. Adagio. 3. Rondo disturbato.
Two-piano version pub. by Schott.

Fanal [Beacon], Op. 45 (1928)
For large orchestra and organ.
Pub. by Schott.

Symphony for Piano and Orchestra (= **Piano Concerto No. 2**), Op. 61
(1932)
1. Allegro. 2. Lebhaft [Lively]. 3. Adagio. 4. Cyclus variabilis.
Two-piano version pub. by Schott.

Variations on Mozart's "Unser dummer Pöbel meint" (1953)
K.455 freely transcribed for orchestra and piano concertante.
Pub. by Belwin-Mills.

Works for Solo Voice, Chorus and Orchestra

An mein Vaterland [To My Homeland], Op. 23 (1913)
Symphony for large orchestra, organ, soprano solo, mixed and boys' choruses.
1. Allegro molto vivace. 2. Adagio, molto espressivo (Psalm 21). 3. Langsam (text by Anastasius Gruen).
Archive.

Die chinesische Flöte [The Chinese Flute], Op. 29 (1922)
Chamber symphony for 14 solo instruments and soprano; from poems by Hans Bethge.
Pub. by Schott (combined English and German vocal score; revised and edited 1949).

Das Wasser [Water], Op. 53 (1930)
Cantata for tenor, baritone, narrator, chorus and various instruments; from writings by Alfred Döblin.
Pub. by Schott (German vocal score).

Musik für Orchester und eine Baritonstimme nach Worten von Rainer Maria Rilke [Music for Orchestra and Baritone Solo on Poems by Rainer Maria Rilke], Op. 60 (1932)
1. Langsam und sehr zart [Slow and very gentle]. 2. Ruhig, etwas frei [Calm, somewhat free]. 3. Quartett (Andante). 4. Allegro incalzato.
Pub. by Schott (combined German and English vocal score).

Cantata of the Bitter Herbs, Op. 65 (1938)
For soprano, alto, tenor, bass, narrator, chorus and orchestra; words from the Bible (Psalm 126); text assembled by Rabbi Jakob Sonderling from the Haggada and other Passover scriptures.
Pub. by Belwin-Mills (English vocal score).

Phantoms, Op. 81 (1957)
For chamber orchestra, speaker and women's speaking chorus; commissioned by radio station Sender Freies Berlin.
1. Poem: "Erlkönig" by J. W. Goethe (in German). 2. Nightpiece. 3. Poem: "The Hag" by Robert Herrick (in English).
Pub. by Belwin-Mills.

Choral Works

Der Tierkreis [The Zodiac], Op. 52 (1930)
For two-part women's chorus.
1. Es sass ein Fuchs [There sat a fox] (Wilhelm Busch). 2. Es sitzt ein Vogel [There sits a bird] (Wilhelm Busch).
Pub. in *Das neue Chorbuch*, Heft 7, Schott.
3. Klapperstorch [Stork] (von Arnim).
Archive.

Gesprochene Musik [Music for Speaking Chorus] (1930)
1. " o a o a o a." 2. "ta tam ta tam ta tam." 3. Fuge aus der Geographie [see next entry].
Archive.

Fuge aus der Geographie [Geographical Fugue] (1930)
For speaking chorus; third movement of *Gesprochene Musik*.
Pub. by Belwin-Mills (separate English and German editions).

The Inner Circle, Op. 67 (1953)
Six a cappella choruses.
1. Cui bono? (Thomas Carlyle). 2. The Lamb (William Blake). 3. Extinguish my eyes (Rainer Maria Rilke). 4. O World, thou chosest not (George Santayana). 5. Have you not heard his silent step (Rabindranath Tagore). 6. Goodbye, proud world (Ralph Waldo Emerson).
Pub. by Belwin-Mills.

Lange schon haben meine Freunde versucht [For a long time now my friends have tried] (1958)
Soprano and baritone duet.
Archive.

Song of Myself (1961)
"I think I could turn and live with animals," from Walt Whitman's *Leaves of Grass*.
Pub. by Belwin-Mills.

Valse for Speaking Chorus and Percussion (1961)
Pub. by Belwin-Mills (separate English and German editions).

Works for Solo Voice and Instruments

Bitte [Request] (c. 1905)
Probably for solo voice and piano.
Lost.

Ich wollt, ich wär ein Fisch [I wish I were a fish] (1920)
For high voice and piano.
Archive.

Neun Lieder für Sopran und Klavier [Nine Songs for Soprano and Piano], Op. 41 (1926) ; English translation by Basil Swift.
1. Der Abend [The Evening] (R. M. Rilke). 2. Heilige [Saints] (Rilke). 3. Die Strassburger Münster-Engelchen [The Angels of the Strasbourg Cathedral] (Otto Julius Bierbaum). 4. Kleine Geschichte [Little Story] (Christian Morgenstern). 5. Spätnachmittag [Late Afternoon] (Kuckuck). 6. Spruch [Saying] (Kuckuck). 7. Was denkst du jetzt? [What do you think now?] (Morgenstern). 8. Das Häuschen an der Bahn [The Little House by the Tracks] (Morgenstern). 9. Der Esel [The Donkey] (Wilhelm Busch).
Pub. by Schott.

Poems to Martha, Op. 66 (1942)
Quintet for strings and medium voice; commissioned by Joseph Haft (who wrote the text) in memory of his wife Martha.
1. Eventide. 2. In the Train. 3. Spring. 4. Farewell.
Pub. by MCA Music (Leeds).

There Is a Season for Everything (1953)
For mezzo-soprano, flute, clarinet, violin and violoncello; words from Ecclesiastes; commissioned by The Baron de Rothschild Foundation for Arts and Sciences.
Pub. by Belwin-Mills.

Vanity of Vanities, All Is Vanity, Op. 79 (1954)
For flute, clarinet, violin, viola, violoncello, soprano and tenor; words from Ecclesiastes; commissioned by the University of Judaism, Los Angeles.
Pub. by Belwin-Mills.

Chamber Music for Wind Instruments

Sonata for Clarinet and Piano, Op. 8 (c. 1905?)
Lost.

Sonata for Clarinet and Piano in A Major, Op. 22 (c. 1913)
Lost.

Tanz-Suite [Dance Suite], Op. 30 (1924)
For flute, clarinet, percussion, violin, viola and double bass (solo instruments).
1. Anstürmend [Stormy]. 2. Schwer, lastend [Heavy, oppressive]. 3. Intermezzo. 4. Gemessen [Sedately]. 5. Intermezzo. 6. Mässig [Moderate].
Pub. by Schott.

Adagio Elegiaco (on the name Fuchs; 1950)
For clarinet and piano.
Archive.

Five Pieces for Wind Instruments and Percussion, Op. 83 (1959)
For flute, oboe, clarinet, bassoon and two horns.
1. Canzonetta. 2. Caprice. 3. Night Song. 4. Roundelay. 5. Cavalcade.
Pub. by Belwin-Mills.

Sonatinetta, Op. 84 (1959)
For flute, clarinet and bassoon; commissioned by RIAS, Berlin.
1. Allegretto comodo. 2. Slow with utmost tenderness. 3. Allegro.
Pub. by Belwin-Mills.

Quartet for Oboe, Clarinet, Bassoon and Viola, Op. 98 (1964)
1. (No tempo indication). 2. Andante cantabile. 3. Allegro molto animato.
Pub. by Belwin-Mills.

Chamber Music for Piano with Strings

Trio for Piano, Violin and Violoncello in D Major (c. 1903)
1. Allegro appassionato. 2. (No tempo indication). 3. Rondo.
Lost.

Vom sterbenden Rokoko [From the Dying Rococo], Op. 16 (1909)
Three pieces for violin and piano.
1. Der Liebestrank [The Love Potion]. 2. Blanchefleure. 3. Madame Dorette.
Archive.

Romanze (c. 1910)
Arrangement for violin and piano of No. 4 of Op. 9 (*Melodische Skizzen,* for piano).
Archive.

Sonata for Violin and Piano, Op. 21 (1912)
1. Allegro non troppo. 2. Adagio non troppo. 3. Allegro giocoso.
Archive.

Sonata for Violin and Piano, Op. 44 (1928)
1. Trotzig, anstürmend [Defiant, stormy]. 2. Intermezzo. 3. Allegro giusto.
Pub. by Schott.

Sonata for Violoncello and Piano, Op. 50 (1929)
1. Allegro comodo. 2. Intermezzo (Die Spinne) [The Spider]. 3. Allegro.
Pub. by Schott.

Piano Quintet, Op. 64 (1938)
Commissioned by Mrs. Elizabeth Sprague Coolidge.
1. Allegro non troppo ("the lyrical part"). 2. Scherzo ("the whimsical part"). 3. Adagio ("the contemplative part"). 4. Allegro ("the dramatic part").
Pub. by MCA Music (Leeds).

String Quartets

String Quartet No. 1 in G Major, Op. 1 (c. 1902)
Lost.

String Quartet No. 2 in D Minor, Op. 2 (c. 1902)
Lost.

String Quartet No. 3 in G Major, Op. 3 (1903)
Andante – Allegro con brio (probably in one movement).
Lost.

String Quartet No. 4 in E-flat Major, Op. 4 (c. 1903)
Lost.

String Quartet No. 5 in C Major, Op. 5 (c. 1903)
Lost.

String Quartet No. 6 in A Minor, Op. 12 (1905)
1. Allegro tranquillo, sempre espressivo. 2. Andantino cantabile. 3. Andante doloroso. 4. Molto vivace e capriccioso.
Archive.

String Quartet No. 7 in G Major, Op. 15 (1908)
1. Allegro piacevole. 2. Andantino cantabile. 3. Vivace. 4. Allegro poco vivace.
Archive.

String Quartet No. 8 in D-flat Major, Op. 18 (1911)
Quasi prologus. 1. Vivace. 2. Andante. 3. Allegro giocoso. 4. Allegro impetuoso ed appassionata [*sic*].
Archive.

String Quartet No. 9 in C Major, Op. 26 (1919)
1. Mit Kraft und ungestüm [Forceful with impetus]. 2. Grazioso. 3. Adagio. 4. Übermütig [Gay and spirited].
Archive.

String Quartet No. 10 on the Name "Bass," Op. 28 (1920)
1. Energisch [With energy]. 2. Adagio molto. 3. Katzenhaft schleichend, geheimnisvoll [Sneakingly, catlike]. 4. Vivace.
Archive.

String Quartet No. 11, Op. 34 (1924)
1. Sehr wuchtig (anstürmend) [Very vigorous (stormy)]. 2. Vivace molto. 3. Adagio. 4. Allegro molto.
Study score pub. by Schott.

String Quartet No. 12, Op. 70 (1946)
1. Calmly and evenly flowing. 2. Adagio. 3. Pensive Serenade. 4. With vigor.
Study score pub. by MCA Music (Leeds).

Dedication (1948)
For string quartet or string orchestra; a short wedding march.
Pub. by Belwin-Mills.

String Quartet No. 13, Op. 74 (1953)
Commissioned by the Coleman Chamber Music Association, Pasadena, for their fiftieth anniversary.
1. Molto tranquillo – Allegro. 2. Allegro non troppo, molto leggiero e grazioso. 3. Lento, dolcissimo con espressione. 4. Allegro assai.
Pub. by Belwin-Mills.

Solos, Duos and Trios for Strings

Duos for Two Violins, Op. 17 (1909)
Open strings only in the pupil's part.

1. Andante. 2. Adagio, ma non troppo. 3. Tempo di minuetto. 4. Allegro giocoso.
Pub. by Belwin-Mills.

Serenade for Three Violins, Op. 20 (1912)
1. Allegro non troppo. 2. Andante. 3. Vivo.
Pub. by Belwin-Mills.

"Spitzweg" Serenade (for Two Violins and Viola), Op. 25 (1917)
Allegro moderato.
Study score pub. by MCA Music (Leeds).

Two Divertimenti for String Duos, Op. 37 (1926)
No. 1. For violin and violoncello. 1. Flott [Lively]. 2. Fliessend [Flowing]. 3. Frisch [Spirited].
No. 2. For violin and viola. 1. Vivace molto. 2. Adagio. 3. Flott und lustig [Lively and merry].
Pub. separately by Schott.

Two Etudes for Violoncello Solo (1930)
1. Andante espressivo. 2. Allegro.
Pub. in *Neue Etüden-Sammlung für Violoncell* (Vol. 15, Nos. 5 & 19), Schott.
Archive.

Two Etudes for Violin Solo (1931)
Lost.

String Trio, Op. 63 (1936)
For violin, viola and violoncello.
1. Allegro. 2. Adagio. 3. Allegro.
Study score pub. by Associated Music Publishers.

Three Impromptus, Op. 90 (1963)
1. Violin solo, Op. 90a. 2. Viola solo, Op. 90b. 3. Violoncello solo, Op. 90c.
Pub. by Belwin-Mills.

Piano Music for Two Hands

Melodische Skizzen [Melodic Sketches], Op. 9 (1903)
1. Ständchen [Serenade]. 2. Reigen [Round Dance]. 3. Scherzetto. 4. Romanze. 5. Papillons.
Archive.

Drei Präludien [Three Preludes], Op. 10 (1903)
1. Allegro moderato. 2. Allegro. 3. Vivace con fuoco.
Archive.

Impromptu (1904)
Lost.

Capriccio (1905)
Lost.

Sonata in C-sharp Minor, Op. 6 (1905)
Lost.

Sonata in D Major, Op. 7 (1905)
Lost.

Stammbuchverse [Album Verses], Op. 13 (1905)
1. Molto moderato e grazioso. 2. Allegretto grazioso. 3. Allegro giusto.
4. Allegro molto moderato. 5. Munter [Gay].
Archive.

Begegnung [Meeting] (1908)
Allegro grazioso.
Archive.

Reminiszenzen, Op. 14 (1909)
1. Allegro non troppo. 2. Leidenschaftlich [Passionately].
Archive.

Vier Klavierstücke [Four Pieces for Piano], Op. 24 (c. 1914)
Lost.

Canon (1915)
Lento, con dolore.
Archive.

Burlesken, Op. 31 (1923)
1. Gemächlich [Easygoing]. 2. Lebhaft [Lively]. 3. Der Jongleur [The
Juggler].
Pub. by Schott.
* No. 3 is also pub. separately.

Drei Klavierstücke [Three Pieces for Piano], Op. 32 (1925)
1. Ruhig und durchweg sehr zart [Calm, and very gentle throughout].
2. Zart, nicht eilen [Gently, without hurrying]. 3. Mässiges Allegro
[Moderate allegro].
Pub. by Schott.

Fünf Capriccetti, Op. 36 (1925)
1. Zart, nachdenklich [Gentle, reflective]. 2. Lebhaft [Lively]. 3. Gra-

ziös, heiter [Graceful, cheerful]. 4. Sehr zart und innig [Very gentle and tender]. 5. Mit ausgelassenem Humor [With exuberant humor].
Pub. by Schott.

Drei Originalstücke für das elektrische Welte-Mignon Klavier [Three Original Pieces for the Welte-Mignon Automatic Piano] (1926)
Commissioned by the Donaueschingen Music Festival.
Archive.

Tanz- und Spielstücke [Pieces for Dancing and Playing], Op. 40 (1927)
1. Grauer Himmel [Gray Skies]. 2. Andante. 3. Sonnenspiel [Sun Game]. 4. Andante. 5. Allegro. 6. Allegro moderato. 7. Allegretto. 8. Allegretto. 9. Allegro. 10. Tanz für Ruth [Dance for Ruth]. 11. Moderato, grazioso. 12. Allegro non troppo. 13. Wetterleuchten [Summer Lightning]. 14. Jazz-Tempo. 15. Jazz-Tempo.
Pub. by Schott.

Studie (1927)
Scored for mechanical organ.
Commissioned by Baden-Baden Music Festival.
Archive.

Sonata, Op. 47 (1928)
1. Quasi Toccata. 2. Intermezzo. 3. Allegro.
Pub. by Schott.

Kleinstadtbilder; vierzehn leichte Stücke [Echoes from a Small Town; Fourteen Easy Pieces], Op. 49 (1929)
1. Junges Kätzchen [Young Kitten]. 2. Müde bin ich [I'm tired]. 3. Ach hätt ich doch [Oh, if I only had]. 4. Auf dem Schulweg [On the Way to School]. 5. Leiermann [Organ Grinder]. 6. Im Gänsemarsch [Follow the Leader]. 7. Armes Kind [Poor Child]. 8. Abzählen [Counting Out]. 9. Spassvogel [Joker]. 10. Alleingelassen [Left Alone]. 11. Hinter der Musik her [Following the Street Band]. 12. Über den Marktplatz [Across the Market Square]. 13. Dem Herbst entgegen [Getting On Toward Autumn]. 14. Gassenhauer [Cheap Popular Song].
Pub. by Schott.

Fünfmal Zehn Etüden [Five Times Ten Etudes] (1931)
10 Konzert-Etüden, Op. 55
10 Vortrags-Etüden [Performance Etudes], Op. 56
10 Mittelstufen-Etüden [Intermediate-Level Etudes], Op. 57
10 einfache Etüden [Simple Etudes], Op. 58
10 Anfangs-Etüden [Etudes for Beginners], Op. 59
Pub. by Schott.

Chansons sans paroles [Songs Without Words] (c. 1940)
Three short untitled pieces in the idiom of the American popular song.
Archive.

Profiles, Op. 68 (1946)
1. Calm. 2. Moderato. 3. Calm, fluent, tender. 4. Merry. 5. Slow, pensive,
very tender. 6. Vigorous, in a hammering way.
Pub. by Associated Music Publishers.

Ideas, Op. 69 (1946)
1. Calm. 2. A black dot dances in my closed eyes. 3. Vivo. 4. Allegro.
Pub. by MCA Music (Leeds).

Diversions, Op. 78a (1956)
1. Andante semplice. 2. Allegro. 3. Tranquillo. 4. Leggiero. 5. Slow, con
molto [*sic*] espressione.
Pub. by MCA Music (Leeds).

Sonatinetta, Op. 78b (1956)
1. Allegro. 2. Andante semplice. 3. Allegro.
Pub. by MCA Music (Leeds).

Miniature Canon ("To Rennie, on his birthday"; 1959)
Archive.

Three Little Dances, Op. 85 (1961)
1. Molto staccato, sempre molto grazioso (all on black keys). 2. A staccato
piece (all on white keys). 3. Lively, vigorous (on mixed keys).
Pub. by Belwin-Mills.

Reflections; Five Pieces for Piano, Op. 86 (1961)
1. (No tempo indication). 2. Allegretto. 3. Allegretto grazioso. 4. Pensive, andante. 5. (No tempo indication).
Pub. by Belwin-Mills.

Piano Music for Four Hands

Sonata, Op. 87 (1962)
1. Allegretto. 2. Andante espressivo. 3. Allegretto amabile, leggiero.
Pub. by Belwin-Mills.

Arrangements and Orchestrations

Eleven Folksong Settings for the "Volksliederbuch für die Jugend" (c.
1930)

For various choral and orchestral combinations.
Archive.

Two Folksong Arrangements for "Folk Songs of the New Palestine" (1938)
For voice and piano.
1. Avatiach [Watermelon]. 2. Tapuach zahav [Orange].
Archive.

Orchestration of Mozart's Sonata K.284 (c. 1945?)
Lost.

Orchestration of Mozart's Sonata K.372 (c. 1945?)
Lost.

Orchestration of Beethoven's Sonata Op. 2, No. 3 (c. 1945?)
Lost.

Orchestration of Beethoven's Sonata Op. 10, No. 3 (c. 1945?)
Lost.

Three Folk Dance Arrangements (1946/47)
For chorus and orchestra; composed for phonograph recordings; score lost; other composers involved in the project included Milhaud, Bernstein and Castelnuovo-Tedesco.
1. Al hasela [On the Rock]. 2. Y'minah y'minah [To the Right]. 3. Yom tov lanu [A Holiday for Us].
Archive.

Incidental Music for Stage Plays

Der Kinder Neujahrstraum [The Children's New Year's Dream], Op. 19 (1910)
Play by Marie Waldeck; never performed.
Archive.

Bacchae (c. 1926)
Berthold Viertel's version of Euripides' play; Mannheim production.
Lost (but part of this became the "Idyll" in the *Spiel für Blasorchester*, Op. 39).

Das Kirschblütenfest [The Cherry Blossom Festival] (1928)
Play by Klabund; Hamburg production.
Pub. by Schott.

As You Like It (1930)
Play by William Shakespeare; Habima (Yiddish theater) production in Berlin.
Lost.

Die Heilige von U.S.A. [The Saint of the U.S.A.] (1931)
Play by Ilse Langner; Berlin production.
Archive.

Uli Wittewüpp (1932)
Play by Marcel Gero; Leipzig production.
Archive.

William Tell (1939)
Play by Friedrich Schiller; Leopold Jessner's production with the Continental Players (a group of German émigrés) in Los Angeles.
Archive.

Incidental Music for Radio Plays

NOTE: Most of these plays were produced by Berliner Rundfunk; *The Gates of Carven Jade* went over the BBC.

Turandot (1930)
Play by Alfred Wolfenstein.
Archive.

Die Räuber [The Robbers] (1931?)
Based on the play by Friedrich Schiller.
Archive.

Die Rollen des Schauspielers Seami [The Roles of the Actor Seami] (1931)
Author unknown.
Archive.

Medea (1931)
Heinz Lipmann's version of Euripides' play.
Archive.

Im fernen Osten [In the Far East] (1931)
Radio play by Gerhard Mengel.
Archive.

König Ödipus [Oedipus Rex] (1931)
Heinz Lipmann's version of Sophocles' play (2 broadcasts: I & II).
Archive.

Anabasis (1931)
Play by Wolfgang Weyrauch, based on Xenophon.
Archive.

Napoleon, oder die hundert Tage [Napoleon, or The Hundred Days] (1932)
Based on the play by Christian Dietrich Grabbe.
Archive.

The Gates of Carven Jade (1934)
Play by C. M. Franzero.
Archive.

Film Scores

Die Kinderfabrik [The Children Factory] (1928)
An experimental project as part of the Deutsches Kammermusikfest in Baden-Baden, whose theme that year was "Film and Music."
Score lost.

Karamazov (a Terra production, Berlin; 1930)
Score lost.

Catherine the Great (London Films-UA; 1934)
Score lost.

The Private Life of Don Juan (London Films-UA; 1934)
Score lost.

Little Friend (Gaumont-British; 1934)
Score lost.

Peter Ibbetson (Paramount; 1935)

Outcast (Paramount; 1937)

On Such a Night (Paramount; 1937)

The Cat and the Canary (Paramount; 1939)

Dr. Cyclops (Paramount; 1940)

The Ghost Breakers (Paramount; 1940)

Ladies in Retirement (Columbia, 1941)

First Comes Courage (Columbia, 1943)

None Shall Escape (Columbia, 1944)

Address Unknown (Columbia, 1944)

The Unseen (Paramount, 1945)

(This listing does not include isolated sequences or unacknowledged contributions in numerous other films. Note that the Warner Bros. film for which Toch originally went to California never materialized.)

INDEX OF NAMES

A CATALOG OF SELECTED
DOVER BOOKS
IN ALL FIELDS OF INTEREST

A CATALOG OF SELECTED DOVER
BOOKS IN ALL FIELDS OF INTEREST

DRAWINGS OF REMBRANDT, edited by Seymour Slive. Updated Lippmann, Hofstede de Groot edition, with definitive scholarly apparatus. All portraits, biblical sketches, landscapes, nudes. Oriental figures, classical studies, together with selection of work by followers. 550 illustrations. Total of 630pp. 9⅛ × 12¼.
21485-0, 21486-9 Pa., Two-vol. set $29.90

GHOST AND HORROR STORIES OF AMBROSE BIERCE, Ambrose Bierce. 24 tales vividly imagined, strangely prophetic, and decades ahead of their time in technical skill: "The Damned Thing," "An Inhabitant of Carcosa," "The Eyes of the Panther," "Moxon's Master," and 20 more. 199pp. 5⅜ × 8½. 20767-6 Pa. $3.95

ETHICAL WRITINGS OF MAIMONIDES, Maimonides. Most significant ethical works of great medieval sage, newly translated for utmost precision, readability. Laws Concerning Character Traits, Eight Chapters, more. 192pp. 5⅜ × 8½.
24522-5 Pa. $4.50

THE EXPLORATION OF THE COLORADO RIVER AND ITS CANYONS, J. W. Powell. Full text of Powell's 1,000-mile expedition down the fabled Colorado in 1869. Superb account of terrain, geology, vegetation, Indians, famine, mutiny, treacherous rapids, mighty canyons, during exploration of last unknown part of continental U.S. 400pp. 5⅜ × 8½. 20094-9 Pa. $7.95

HISTORY OF PHILOSOPHY, Julián Marías. Clearest one-volume history on the market. Every major philosopher and dozens of others, to Existentialism and later. 505pp. 5⅜ × 8½. 21739-6 Pa. $9.95

ALL ABOUT LIGHTNING, Martin A. Uman. Highly readable non-technical survey of nature and causes of lightning, thunderstorms, ball lightning, St. Elmo's Fire, much more. Illustrated. 192pp. 5⅜ × 8½. 25237-X Pa. $5.95

SAILING ALONE AROUND THE WORLD, Captain Joshua Slocum. First man to sail around the world, alone, in small boat. One of great feats of seamanship told in delightful manner. 67 illustrations. 294pp. 5⅜ × 8½. 20326-3 Pa. $4.95

LETTERS AND NOTES ON THE MANNERS, CUSTOMS AND CONDITIONS OF THE NORTH AMERICAN INDIANS, George Catlin. Classic account of life among Plains Indians: ceremonies, hunt, warfare, etc. 312 plates. 572pp. of text. 6⅛ × 9¼. 22118-0, 22119-9, Pa. Two-vol. set $17.90

ALASKA: The Harriman Expedition, 1899, John Burroughs, John Muir, et al. Informative, engrossing accounts of two-month, 9,000-mile expedition. Native peoples, wildlife, forests, geography, salmon industry, glaciers, more. Profusely illustrated. 240 black-and-white line drawings. 124 black-and-white photographs. 3 maps. Index. 576pp. 5⅜ × 8½. 25109-8 Pa. $11.95

THE BOOK OF BEASTS: Being a Translation from a Latin Bestiary of the Twelfth Century, T. H. White. Wonderful catalog real and fanciful beasts: manticore, griffin, phoenix, amphivius, jaculus, many more. White's witty erudite commentary on scientific, historical aspects. Fascinating glimpse of medieval mind. Illustrated. 296pp. 5⅜ × 8¼. (Available in U.S. only) 24609-4 Pa. $6.95

FRANK LLOYD WRIGHT: ARCHITECTURE AND NATURE With 160 Illustrations, Donald Hoffmann. Profusely illustrated study of influence of nature—especially prairie—on Wright's designs for Fallingwater, Robie House, Guggenheim Museum, other masterpieces. 96pp. 9¼ × 10¾. 25098-9 Pa. $7.95

FRANK LLOYD WRIGHT'S FALLINGWATER, Donald Hoffmann. Wright's famous waterfall house: planning and construction of organic idea. History of site, owners, Wright's personal involvement. Photographs of various stages of building. Preface by Edgar Kaufmann, Jr. 100 illustrations. 112pp. 9¼ × 10.
23671-4 Pa. $8.95

YEARS WITH FRANK LLOYD WRIGHT: Apprentice to Genius, Edgar Tafel. Insightful memoir by a former apprentice presents a revealing portrait of Wright the man, the inspired teacher, the greatest American architect. 372 black-and-white illustrations. Preface. Index. vi + 228pp. 8¼ × 11. 24801-1 Pa. $10.95

THE STORY OF KING ARTHUR AND HIS KNIGHTS, Howard Pyle. Enchanting version of King Arthur fable has delighted generations with imaginative narratives of exciting adventures and unforgettable illustrations by the author. 41 illustrations. xviii + 313pp. 6⅛ × 9¼. 21445-1 Pa. $6.95

THE GODS OF THE EGYPTIANS, E. A. Wallis Budge. Thorough coverage of numerous gods of ancient Egypt by foremost Egyptologist. Information on evolution of cults, rites and gods; the cult of Osiris; the Book of the Dead and its rites; the sacred animals and birds; Heaven and Hell; and more. 956pp. 6⅛ × 9¼.
22055-9, 22056-7 Pa., Two-vol. set $21.90

A THEOLOGICO-POLITICAL TREATISE, Benedict Spinoza. Also contains unfinished *Political Treatise*. Great classic on religious liberty, theory of government on common consent. R. Elwes translation. Total of 421pp. 5⅜ × 8½.
20249-6 Pa. $6.95

INCIDENTS OF TRAVEL IN CENTRAL AMERICA, CHIAPAS, AND YUCATAN, John L. Stephens. Almost single-handed discovery of Maya culture; exploration of ruined cities, monuments, temples; customs of Indians. 115 drawings. 892pp. 5⅜ × 8½. 22404-X, 22405-8 Pa., Two-vol. set $15.90

LOS CAPRICHOS, Francisco Goya. 80 plates of wild, grotesque monsters and caricatures. Prado manuscript included. 183pp. 6⅝ × 9⅜. 22384-1 Pa. $5.95

AUTOBIOGRAPHY: The Story of My Experiments with Truth, Mohandas K. Gandhi. Not hagiography, but Gandhi in his own words. Boyhood, legal studies, purification, the growth of the Satyagraha (nonviolent protest) movement. Critical, inspiring work of the man who freed India. 480pp. 5⅜ × 8½. (Available in U.S. only)
24593-4 Pa. $6.95

ILLUSTRATED DICTIONARY OF HISTORIC ARCHITECTURE, edited by Cyril M. Harris. Extraordinary compendium of clear, concise definitions for over 5,000 important architectural terms complemented by over 2,000 line drawings. Covers full spectrum of architecture from ancient ruins to 20th-century Modernism. Preface. 592pp. 7½ × 9⅜. 24444-X Pa. $15.95

THE NIGHT BEFORE CHRISTMAS, Clement Moore. Full text, and woodcuts from original 1848 book. Also critical, historical material. 19 illustrations. 40pp. 4⅝ × 6. 22797-9 Pa. $2.50

THE LESSON OF JAPANESE ARCHITECTURE: 165 Photographs, Jiro Harada. Memorable gallery of 165 photographs taken in the 1930's of exquisite Japanese homes of the well-to-do and historic buildings. 13 line diagrams. 192pp. 8⅜ × 11¼. 24778-3 Pa. $10.95

THE AUTOBIOGRAPHY OF CHARLES DARWIN AND SELECTED LETTERS, edited by Francis Darwin. The fascinating life of eccentric genius composed of an intimate memoir by Darwin (intended for his children); commentary by his son, Francis; hundreds of fragments from notebooks, journals, papers; and letters to and from Lyell, Hooker, Huxley, Wallace and Henslow. xi + 365pp. 5⅜ × 8. 20479-0 Pa. $6.95

WONDERS OF THE SKY: Observing Rainbows, Comets, Eclipses, the Stars and Other Phenomena, Fred Schaaf. Charming, easy-to-read poetic guide to all manner of celestial events visible to the naked eye. Mock suns, glories, Belt of Venus, more. Illustrated. 299pp. 5¼ × 8¼. 24402-4 Pa. $7.95

BURNHAM'S CELESTIAL HANDBOOK, Robert Burnham, Jr. Thorough guide to the stars beyond our solar system. Exhaustive treatment. Alphabetical by constellation: Andromeda to Cetus in Vol. 1; Chamaeleon to Orion in Vol. 2; and Pavo to Vulpecula in Vol. 3. Hundreds of illustrations. Index in Vol. 3. 2,000pp. 6⅛ × 9¼. 23567-X, 23568-8, 23673-0 Pa., Three-vol. set $38.85

STAR NAMES: Their Lore and Meaning, Richard Hinckley Allen. Fascinating history of names various cultures have given to constellations and literary and folkloristic uses that have been made of stars. Indexes to subjects. Arabic and Greek names. Biblical references. Bibliography. 563pp. 5⅜ × 8½. 21079-0 Pa. $8.95

THIRTY YEARS THAT SHOOK PHYSICS: The Story of Quantum Theory, George Gamow. Lucid, accessible introduction to influential theory of energy and matter. Careful explanations of Dirac's anti-particles, Bohr's model of the atom, much more. 12 plates. Numerous drawings. 240pp. 5⅜ × 8½. 24895-X Pa. $5.95

CHINESE DOMESTIC FURNITURE IN PHOTOGRAPHS AND MEASURED DRAWINGS, Gustav Ecke. A rare volume, now affordably priced for antique collectors, furniture buffs and art historians. Detailed review of styles ranging from early Shang to late Ming. Unabridged republication. 161 black-and-white drawings, photos. Total of 224pp. 8⅜ × 11¼. (Available in U.S. only) 25171-3 Pa. $13.95

VINCENT VAN GOGH: A Biography, Julius Meier-Graefe. Dynamic, penetrating study of artist's life, relationship with brother, Theo, painting techniques, travels, more. Readable, engrossing. 160pp. 5⅜ × 8½. (Available in U.S. only) 25253-1 Pa. $4.95

HOW TO WRITE, Gertrude Stein. Gertrude Stein claimed anyone could understand her unconventional writing—here are clues to help. Fascinating improvisations, language experiments, explanations illuminate Stein's craft and the art of writing. Total of 414pp. 4⅜ × 6⅜. 23144-5 Pa. $6.95

ADVENTURES AT SEA IN THE GREAT AGE OF SAIL: Five Firsthand Narratives, edited by Elliot Snow. Rare true accounts of exploration, whaling, shipwreck, fierce natives, trade, shipboard life, more. 33 illustrations. Introduction. 353pp. 5⅜ × 8½. 25177-2 Pa. $8.95

THE HERBAL OR GENERAL HISTORY OF PLANTS, John Gerard. Classic descriptions of about 2,850 plants—with over 2,700 illustrations—includes Latin and English names, physical descriptions, varieties, time and place of growth, more. 2,706 illustrations. xlv + 1,678pp. 8½ × 12¼. 23147-X Cloth. $75.00

DOROTHY AND THE WIZARD IN OZ, L. Frank Baum. Dorothy and the Wizard visit the center of the Earth, where people are vegetables, glass houses grow and Oz characters reappear. Classic sequel to *Wizard of Oz*. 256pp. 5⅜ × 8. 24714-7 Pa. $4.95

SONGS OF EXPERIENCE: Facsimile Reproduction with 26 Plates in Full Color, William Blake. This facsimile of Blake's original "Illuminated Book" reproduces 26 full-color plates from a rare 1826 edition. Includes "The Tyger," "London," "Holy Thursday," and other immortal poems. 26 color plates. Printed text of poems. 48pp. 5¼ × 7. 24636-1 Pa. $3.50

SONGS OF INNOCENCE, William Blake. The first and most popular of Blake's famous "Illuminated Books," in a facsimile edition reproducing all 31 brightly colored plates. Additional printed text of each poem. 64pp. 5¼ × 7. 22764-2 Pa. $3.50

PRECIOUS STONES, Max Bauer. Classic, thorough study of diamonds, rubies, emeralds, garnets, etc.: physical character, occurrence, properties, use, similar topics. 20 plates, 8 in color. 94 figures. 659pp. 6⅛ × 9¼. 21910-0, 21911-9 Pa., Two-vol. set $15.90

ENCYCLOPEDIA OF VICTORIAN NEEDLEWORK, S. F. A. Caulfeild and Blanche Saward. Full, precise descriptions of stitches, techniques for dozens of needlecrafts—most exhaustive reference of its kind. Over 800 figures. Total of 679pp. 8⅛ × 11. Two volumes. Vol. 1 22800-2 Pa. $11.95
Vol. 2 22801-0 Pa. $11.95

THE MARVELOUS LAND OF OZ, L. Frank Baum. Second Oz book, the Scarecrow and Tin Woodman are back with hero named Tip, Oz magic. 136 illustrations. 287pp. 5⅜ × 8½. 20692-0 Pa. $5.95

WILD FOWL DECOYS, Joel Barber. Basic book on the subject, by foremost authority and collector. Reveals history of decoy making and rigging, place in American culture, different kinds of decoys, how to make them, and how to use them. 140 plates. 156pp. 7⅞ × 10¾. 20011-6 Pa. $8.95

HISTORY OF LACE, Mrs. Bury Palliser. Definitive, profusely illustrated chronicle of lace from earliest times to late 19th century. Laces of Italy, Greece, England, France, Belgium, etc. Landmark of needlework scholarship. 266 illustrations. 672pp. 6⅛ × 9¼. 24742-2 Pa. $14.95

ILLUSTRATED GUIDE TO SHAKER FURNITURE, Robert Meader. All furniture and appurtenances, with much on unknown local styles. 235 photos. 146pp. 9 × 12. 22819-3 Pa. $8.95

WHALE SHIPS AND WHALING: A Pictorial Survey, George Francis Dow. Over 200 vintage engravings, drawings, photographs of barks, brigs, cutters, other vessels. Also harpoons, lances, whaling guns, many other artifacts. Comprehensive text by foremost authority. 207 black-and-white illustrations. 288pp. 6 × 9. 24808-9 Pa. $8.95

THE BERTRAMS, Anthony Trollope. Powerful portrayal of blind self-will and thwarted ambition includes one of Trollope's most heartrending love stories. 497pp. 5⅜ × 8½. 25119-5 Pa. $9.95

ADVENTURES WITH A HAND LENS, Richard Headstrom. Clearly written guide to observing and studying flowers and grasses, fish scales, moth and insect wings, egg cases, buds, feathers, seeds, leaf scars, moss, molds, ferns, common crystals, etc.—all with an ordinary, inexpensive magnifying glass. 209 exact line drawings aid in your discoveries. 220pp. 5⅜ × 8½. 23330-8 Pa. $4.95

RODIN ON ART AND ARTISTS, Auguste Rodin. Great sculptor's candid, wide-ranging comments on meaning of art; great artists; relation of sculpture to poetry, painting, music; philosophy of life, more. 76 superb black-and-white illustrations of Rodin's sculpture, drawings and prints. 119pp. 8⅜ × 11¼. 24487-3 Pa. $7.95

FIFTY CLASSIC FRENCH FILMS, 1912–1982: A Pictorial Record, Anthony Slide. Memorable stills from Grand Illusion, Beauty and the Beast, Hiroshima, Mon Amour, many more. Credits, plot synopses, reviews, etc. 160pp. 8¼ × 11. 25256-6 Pa. $11.95

THE PRINCIPLES OF PSYCHOLOGY, William James. Famous long course complete, unabridged. Stream of thought, time perception, memory, experimental methods; great work decades ahead of its time. 94 figures. 1,391pp. 5⅜ × 8½. 20381-6, 20382-4 Pa., Two-vol. set $23.90

BODIES IN A BOOKSHOP, R. T. Campbell. Challenging mystery of blackmail and murder with ingenious plot and superbly drawn characters. In the best tradition of British suspense fiction. 192pp. 5⅜ × 8½. 24720-1 Pa. $3.95

CALLAS: PORTRAIT OF A PRIMA DONNA, George Jellinek. Renowned commentator on the musical scene chronicles incredible career and life of the most controversial, fascinating, influential operatic personality of our time. 64 black-and-white photographs. 416pp. 5⅜ × 8¼. 25047-4 Pa. $8.95

GEOMETRY, RELATIVITY AND THE FOURTH DIMENSION, Rudolph Rucker. Exposition of fourth dimension, concepts of relativity as Flatland characters continue adventures. Popular, easily followed yet accurate, profound. 141 illustrations. 133pp. 5⅜ × 8½. 23400-2 Pa. $3.95

HOUSEHOLD STORIES BY THE BROTHERS GRIMM, with pictures by Walter Crane. 53 classic stories—Rumpelstiltskin, Rapunzel, Hansel and Gretel, the Fisherman and his Wife, Snow White, Tom Thumb, Sleeping Beauty, Cinderella, and so much more—lavishly illustrated with original 19th century drawings. 114 illustrations. x + 269pp. 5⅜ × 8½. 21080-4 Pa. $4.95

SUNDIALS, Albert Waugh. Far and away the best, most thorough coverage of ideas, mathematics concerned, types, construction, adjusting anywhere. Over 100 illustrations. 230pp. 5⅜ × 8½. 22947-5 Pa. $4.95

PICTURE HISTORY OF THE NORMANDIE: With 190 Illustrations, Frank O. Braynard. Full story of legendary French ocean liner: Art Deco interiors, design innovations, furnishings, celebrities, maiden voyage, tragic fire, much more. Extensive text. 144pp. 8⅞ × 11¾. 25257-4 Pa. $10.95

THE FIRST AMERICAN COOKBOOK: A Facsimile of "American Cookery," 1796, Amelia Simmons. Facsimile of the first American-written cookbook published in the United States contains authentic recipes for colonial favorites—pumpkin pudding, winter squash pudding, spruce beer, Indian slapjacks, and more. Introductory Essay and Glossary of colonial cooking terms. 80pp. 5⅜ × 8½. 24710-4 Pa. $3.50

101 PUZZLES IN THOUGHT AND LOGIC, C. R. Wylie, Jr. Solve murders and robberies, find out which fishermen are liars, how a blind man could possibly identify a color—purely by your own reasoning! 107pp. 5⅜ × 8½. 20367-0 Pa. $2.50

THE BOOK OF WORLD-FAMOUS MUSIC—CLASSICAL, POPULAR AND FOLK, James J. Fuld. Revised and enlarged republication of landmark work in musico-bibliography. Full information about nearly 1,000 songs and compositions including first lines of music and lyrics. New supplement. Index. 800pp. 5⅜ × 8¼. 24857-7 Pa. $15.95

ANTHROPOLOGY AND MODERN LIFE, Franz Boas. Great anthropologist's classic treatise on race and culture. Introduction by Ruth Bunzel. Only inexpensive paperback edition. 255pp. 5⅜ × 8½. 25245-0 Pa. $6.95

THE TALE OF PETER RABBIT, Beatrix Potter. The inimitable Peter's terrifying adventure in Mr. McGregor's garden, with all 27 wonderful, full-color Potter illustrations. 55pp. 4¼ × 5½. (Available in U.S. only) 22827-4 Pa. $1.75

THREE PROPHETIC SCIENCE FICTION NOVELS, H. G. Wells. *When the Sleeper Wakes, A Story of the Days to Come* and *The Time Machine* (full version). 335pp. 5⅜ × 8½. (Available in U.S. only) 20605-X Pa. $6.95

APICIUS COOKERY AND DINING IN IMPERIAL ROME, edited and translated by Joseph Dommers Vehling. Oldest known cookbook in existence offers readers a clear picture of what foods Romans ate, how they prepared them, etc. 49 illustrations. 301pp. 6⅛ × 9¼. 23563-7 Pa. $7.95

SHAKESPEARE LEXICON AND QUOTATION DICTIONARY, Alexander Schmidt. Full definitions, locations, shades of meaning of every word in plays and poems. More than 50,000 exact quotations. 1,485pp. 6½ × 9¼. 22726-X, 22727-8 Pa., Two-vol. set $29.90

THE WORLD'S GREAT SPEECHES, edited by Lewis Copeland and Lawrence W. Lamm. Vast collection of 278 speeches from Greeks to 1970. Powerful and effective models; unique look at history. 842pp. 5⅜ × 8½. 20468-5 Pa. $11.95

THE BLUE FAIRY BOOK, Andrew Lang. The first, most famous collection, with many familiar tales: Little Red Riding Hood, Aladdin and the Wonderful Lamp, Puss in Boots, Sleeping Beauty, Hansel and Gretel, Rumpelstiltskin; 37 in all. 138 illustrations. 390pp. 5⅜ × 8½. 21437-0 Pa. $6.95

THE STORY OF THE CHAMPIONS OF THE ROUND TABLE, Howard Pyle. Sir Launcelot, Sir Tristram and Sir Percival in spirited adventures of love and triumph retold in Pyle's inimitable style. 50 drawings, 31 full-page. xviii + 329pp. 6½ × 9¼. 21883-X Pa. $7.95

AUDUBON AND HIS JOURNALS, Maria Audubon. Unmatched two-volume portrait of the great artist, naturalist and author contains his journals, an excellent biography by his granddaughter, expert annotations by the noted ornithologist, Dr. Elliott Coues, and 37 superb illustrations. Total of 1,200pp. 5⅜ × 8.
Vol. I 25143-8 Pa. $8.95
Vol. II 25144-6 Pa. $8.95

GREAT DINOSAUR HUNTERS AND THEIR DISCOVERIES, Edwin H. Colbert. Fascinating, lavishly illustrated chronicle of dinosaur research, 1820's to 1960. Achievements of Cope, Marsh, Brown, Buckland, Mantell, Huxley, many others. 384pp. 5¼ × 8¼. 24701-5 Pa. $7.95

THE TASTEMAKERS, Russell Lynes. Informal, illustrated social history of American taste 1850's-1950's. First popularized categories Highbrow, Lowbrow, Middlebrow. 129 illustrations. New (1979) afterword. 384pp. 6 × 9.
23993-4 Pa. $8.95

DOUBLE CROSS PURPOSES, Ronald A. Knox. A treasure hunt in the Scottish Highlands, an old map, unidentified corpse, surprise discoveries keep reader guessing in this cleverly intricate tale of financial skullduggery. 2 black-and-white maps. 320pp. 5⅜ × 8½. (Available in U.S. only) 25032-6 Pa. $6.95

AUTHENTIC VICTORIAN DECORATION AND ORNAMENTATION IN FULL COLOR: 46 Plates from "Studies in Design," Christopher Dresser. Superb full-color lithographs reproduced from rare original portfolio of a major Victorian designer. 48pp. 9¼ × 12¼. 25083-0 Pa. $7.95

PRIMITIVE ART, Franz Boas. Remains the best text ever prepared on subject, thoroughly discussing Indian, African, Asian, Australian, and, especially, Northern American primitive art. Over 950 illustrations show ceramics, masks, totem poles, weapons, textiles, paintings, much more. 376pp. 5⅜ × 8. 20025-6 Pa. $6.95

SIDELIGHTS ON RELATIVITY, Albert Einstein. Unabridged republication of two lectures delivered by the great physicist in 1920-21. *Ether and Relativity* and *Geometry and Experience*. Elegant ideas in non-mathematical form, accessible to intelligent layman. vi + 56pp. 5⅜ × 8½. 24511-X Pa. $2.95

THE WIT AND HUMOR OF OSCAR WILDE, edited by Alvin Redman. More than 1,000 ripostes, paradoxes, wisecracks: Work is the curse of the drinking classes, I can resist everything except temptation, etc. 258pp. 5⅜ × 8½. 20602-5 Pa. $4.95

ADVENTURES WITH A MICROSCOPE, Richard Headstrom. 59 adventures with clothing fibers, protozoa, ferns and lichens, roots and leaves, much more. 142 illustrations. 232pp. 5⅜ × 8½. 23471-1 Pa. $3.95

PLANTS OF THE BIBLE, Harold N. Moldenke and Alma L. Moldenke. Standard reference to all 230 plants mentioned in Scriptures. Latin name, biblical reference, uses, modern identity, much more. Unsurpassed encyclopedic resource for scholars, botanists, nature lovers, students of Bible. Bibliography. Indexes. 123 black-and-white illustrations. 384pp. 6 × 9. 25069-5 Pa. $8.95

FAMOUS AMERICAN WOMEN: A Biographical Dictionary from Colonial Times to the Present, Robert McHenry, ed. From Pocahontas to Rosa Parks, 1,035 distinguished American women documented in separate biographical entries. Accurate, up-to-date data, numerous categories, spans 400 years. Indices. 493pp. 6½ × 9¼. 24523-3 Pa. $10.95

THE FABULOUS INTERIORS OF THE GREAT OCEAN LINERS IN HISTORIC PHOTOGRAPHS, William H. Miller, Jr. Some 200 superb photographs capture exquisite interiors of world's great "floating palaces"—1890's to 1980's: *Titanic, Ile de France, Queen Elizabeth, United States, Europa,* more. Approx. 200 black-and-white photographs. Captions. Text. Introduction. 160pp. 8⅞ × 11¾. 24756-2 Pa. $9.95

THE GREAT LUXURY LINERS, 1927–1954: A Photographic Record, William H. Miller, Jr. Nostalgic tribute to heyday of ocean liners. 186 photos of Ile de France, Normandie, Leviathan, Queen Elizabeth, United States, many others. Interior and exterior views. Introduction. Captions. 160pp. 9 × 12. 24056-8 Pa. $10.95

A NATURAL HISTORY OF THE DUCKS, John Charles Phillips. Great landmark of ornithology offers complete detailed coverage of nearly 200 species and subspecies of ducks: gadwall, sheldrake, merganser, pintail, many more. 74 full-color plates, 102 black-and-white. Bibliography. Total of 1,920pp. 8⅝ × 11¼. 25141-1, 25142-X Cloth. Two-vol. set $100.00

THE SEAWEED HANDBOOK: An Illustrated Guide to Seaweeds from North Carolina to Canada, Thomas F. Lee. Concise reference covers 78 species. Scientific and common names, habitat, distribution, more. Finding keys for easy identification. 224pp. 5⅜ × 8½. 25215-9 Pa. $6.95

THE TEN BOOKS OF ARCHITECTURE: The 1755 Leoni Edition, Leon Battista Alberti. Rare classic helped introduce the glories of ancient architecture to the Renaissance. 68 black-and-white plates. 336pp. 8⅜ × 11¼. 25239-6 Pa. $14.95

MISS MACKENZIE, Anthony Trollope. Minor masterpieces by Victorian master unmasks many truths about life in 19th-century England. First inexpensive edition in years. 392pp. 5⅜ × 8½. 25201-9 Pa. $8.95

THE RIME OF THE ANCIENT MARINER, Gustave Doré, Samuel Taylor Coleridge. Dramatic engravings considered by many to be his greatest work. The terrifying space of the open sea, the storms and whirlpools of an unknown ocean, the ice of Antarctica, more—all rendered in a powerful, chilling manner. Full text. 38 plates. 77pp. 9¼ × 12. 22305-1 Pa. $4.95

THE EXPEDITIONS OF ZEBULON MONTGOMERY PIKE, Zebulon Montgomery Pike. Fascinating first-hand accounts (1805–6) of exploration of Mississippi River, Indian wars, capture by Spanish dragoons, much more. 1,088pp. 5⅜ × 8½. 25254-X, 25255-8 Pa. Two-vol. set $25.90

A CONCISE HISTORY OF PHOTOGRAPHY: Third Revised Edition, Helmut Gernsheim. Best one-volume history—camera obscura, photochemistry, daguerreotypes, evolution of cameras, film, more. Also artistic aspects—landscape, portraits, fine art, etc. 281 black-and-white photographs. 26 in color. 176pp. 8⅜ × 11¼. 25128-4 Pa. $13.95

THE DORÉ BIBLE ILLUSTRATIONS, Gustave Doré. 241 detailed plates from the Bible: the Creation scenes, Adam and Eve, Flood, Babylon, battle sequences, life of Jesus, etc. Each plate is accompanied by the verses from the King James version of the Bible. 241pp. 9 × 12. 23004-X Pa. $9.95

HUGGER-MUGGER IN THE LOUVRE, Elliot Paul. Second Homer Evans mystery-comedy. Theft at the Louvre involves sleuth in hilarious, madcap caper. "A knockout."—Books. 336pp. 5⅜ × 8½. 25185-3 Pa. $5.95

FLATLAND, E. A. Abbott. Intriguing and enormously popular science-fiction classic explores the complexities of trying to survive as a two-dimensional being in a three-dimensional world. Amusingly illustrated by the author. 16 illustrations. 103pp. 5⅜ × 8½. 20001-9 Pa. $2.50

THE HISTORY OF THE LEWIS AND CLARK EXPEDITION, Meriwether Lewis and William Clark, edited by Elliott Coues. Classic edition of Lewis and Clark's day-by-day journals that later became the basis for U.S. claims to Oregon and the West. Accurate and invaluable geographical, botanical, biological, meteorological and anthropological material. Total of 1,508pp. 5⅜ × 8½.
21268-8, 21269-6, 21270-X Pa. Three-vol. set $26.85

LANGUAGE, TRUTH AND LOGIC, Alfred J. Ayer. Famous, clear introduction to Vienna, Cambridge schools of Logical Positivism. Role of philosophy, elimination of metaphysics, nature of analysis, etc. 160pp. 5⅜ × 8½. (Available in U.S. and Canada only) 20010-8 Pa. $3.95

MATHEMATICS FOR THE NONMATHEMATICIAN, Morris Kline. Detailed, college-level treatment of mathematics in cultural and historical context, with numerous exercises. For liberal arts students. Preface. Recommended Reading Lists. Tables. Index. Numerous black-and-white figures. xvi + 641pp. 5⅜ × 8½.
24823-2 Pa. $11.95

HANDBOOK OF PICTORIAL SYMBOLS, Rudolph Modley. 3,250 signs and symbols, many systems in full; official or heavy commercial use. Arranged by subject. Most in Pictorial Archive series. 143pp. 8⅛ × 11. 23357-X Pa. $6.95

INCIDENTS OF TRAVEL IN YUCATAN, John L. Stephens. Classic (1843) exploration of jungles of Yucatan, looking for evidences of Maya civilization. Travel adventures, Mexican and Indian culture, etc. Total of 669pp. 5⅜ × 8½.
20926-1, 20927-X Pa., Two-vol. set $11.90

DEGAS: An Intimate Portrait, Ambroise Vollard. Charming, anecdotal memoir by famous art dealer of one of the greatest 19th-century French painters. 14 black-and-white illustrations. Introduction by Harold L. Van Doren. 96pp. 5⅜ × 8½.

25131-4 Pa. $4.95

PERSONAL NARRATIVE OF A PILGRIMAGE TO ALMANDINAH AND MECCAH, Richard Burton. Great travel classic by remarkably colorful personality. Burton, disguised as a Moroccan, visited sacred shrines of Islam, narrowly escaping death. 47 illustrations. 959pp. 5⅜ × 8½. 21217-3, 21218-1 Pa., Two-vol. set $19.90

PHRASE AND WORD ORIGINS, A. H. Holt. Entertaining, reliable, modern study of more than 1,200 colorful words, phrases, origins and histories. Much unexpected information. 254pp. 5⅜ × 8½. 20758-7 Pa. $5.95

THE RED THUMB MARK, R. Austin Freeman. In this first Dr. Thorndyke case, the great scientific detective draws fascinating conclusions from the nature of a single fingerprint. Exciting story, authentic science. 320pp. 5⅜ × 8½. (Available in U.S. only) 25210-8 Pa. $6.95

AN EGYPTIAN HIEROGLYPHIC DICTIONARY, E. A. Wallis Budge. Monumental work containing about 25,000 words or terms that occur in texts ranging from 3000 B.C. to 600 A.D. Each entry consists of a transliteration of the word, the word in hieroglyphs, and the meaning in English. 1,314pp. 6⅝ × 10.

23615-3, 23616-1 Pa., Two-vol. set $31.90

THE COMPLEAT STRATEGYST: Being a Primer on the Theory of Games of Strategy, J. D. Williams. Highly entertaining classic describes, with many illustrated examples, how to select best strategies in conflict situations. Prefaces. Appendices. xvi + 268pp. 5⅜ × 8½. 25101-2 Pa. $5.95

THE ROAD TO OZ, L. Frank Baum. Dorothy meets the Shaggy Man, little Button-Bright and the Rainbow's beautiful daughter in this delightful trip to the magical Land of Oz. 272pp. 5⅜ × 8. 25208-6 Pa. $5.95

POINT AND LINE TO PLANE, Wassily Kandinsky. Seminal exposition of role of point, line, other elements in non-objective painting. Essential to understanding 20th-century art. 127 illustrations. 192pp. 6½ × 9¼. 23808-3 Pa. $4.95

LADY ANNA, Anthony Trollope. Moving chronicle of Countess Lovel's bitter struggle to win for herself and daughter Anna their rightful rank and fortune—perhaps at cost of sanity itself. 384pp. 5⅜ × 8½. 24669-8 Pa. $8.95

EGYPTIAN MAGIC, E. A. Wallis Budge. Sums up all that is known about magic in Ancient Egypt: the role of magic in controlling the gods, powerful amulets that warded off evil spirits, scarabs of immortality, use of wax images, formulas and spells, the secret name, much more. 253pp. 5⅜ × 8½. 22681-6 Pa. $4.50

THE DANCE OF SIVA, Ananda Coomaraswamy. Preeminent authority unfolds the vast metaphysic of India: the revelation of her art, conception of the universe, social organization, etc. 27 reproductions of art masterpieces. 192pp. 5⅜ × 8½.

24817-8 Pa. $5.95

CHRISTMAS CUSTOMS AND TRADITIONS, Clement A. Miles. Origin, evolution, significance of religious, secular practices. Caroling, gifts, yule logs, much more. Full, scholarly yet fascinating; non-sectarian. 400pp. 5⅜ × 8½.
23354-5 Pa. $6.95

THE HUMAN FIGURE IN MOTION, Eadweard Muybridge. More than 4,500 stopped-action photos, in action series, showing undraped men, women, children jumping, lying down, throwing, sitting, wrestling, carrying, etc. 390pp. 7⅞ × 10⅝.
20204-6 Cloth. $21.95

THE MAN WHO WAS THURSDAY, Gilbert Keith Chesterton. Witty, fast-paced novel about a club of anarchists in turn-of-the-century London. Brilliant social, religious, philosophical speculations. 128pp. 5⅜ × 8½.
25121-7 Pa. $3.95

A CEZANNE SKETCHBOOK: Figures, Portraits, Landscapes and Still Lifes, Paul Cezanne. Great artist experiments with tonal effects, light, mass, other qualities in over 100 drawings. A revealing view of developing master painter, precursor of Cubism. 102 black-and-white illustrations. 144pp. 8¾ × 6⅜.
24790-2 Pa. $5.95

AN ENCYCLOPEDIA OF BATTLES: Accounts of Over 1,560 Battles from 1479 B.C. to the Present, David Eggenberger. Presents essential details of every major battle in recorded history, from the first battle of Megiddo in 1479 B.C. to Grenada in 1984. List of Battle Maps. New Appendix covering the years 1967–1984. Index. 99 illustrations. 544pp. 6½ × 9¼.
24913-1 Pa. $14.95

AN ETYMOLOGICAL DICTIONARY OF MODERN ENGLISH, Ernest Weekley. Richest, fullest work, by foremost British lexicographer. Detailed word histories. Inexhaustible. Total of 856pp. 6½ × 9¼.
21873-2, 21874-0 Pa., Two-vol. set $17.00

WEBSTER'S AMERICAN MILITARY BIOGRAPHIES, edited by Robert McHenry. Over 1,000 figures who shaped 3 centuries of American military history. Detailed biographies of Nathan Hale, Douglas MacArthur, Mary Hallaren, others. Chronologies of engagements, more. Introduction. Addenda. 1,033 entries in alphabetical order. xi + 548pp. 6½ × 9¼. (Available in U.S. only)
24758-9 Pa. $13.95

LIFE IN ANCIENT EGYPT, Adolf Erman. Detailed older account, with much not in more recent books: domestic life, religion, magic, medicine, commerce, and whatever else needed for complete picture. Many illustrations. 597pp. 5⅜ × 8½.
22632-8 Pa. $8.95

HISTORIC COSTUME IN PICTURES, Braun & Schneider. Over 1,450 costumed figures shown, covering a wide variety of peoples: kings, emperors, nobles, priests, servants, soldiers, scholars, townsfolk, peasants, merchants, courtiers, cavaliers, and more. 256pp. 8⅜ × 11¼.
23150-X Pa. $9.95

THE NOTEBOOKS OF LEONARDO DA VINCI, edited by J. P. Richter. Extracts from manuscripts reveal great genius; on painting, sculpture, anatomy, sciences, geography, etc. Both Italian and English. 186 ms. pages reproduced, plus 500 additional drawings, including studies for *Last Supper, Sforza* monument, etc. 860pp. 7⅞ × 10¾. (Available in U.S. only) 22572-0, 22573-9 Pa., Two-vol. set $31.90

THE ART NOUVEAU STYLE BOOK OF ALPHONSE MUCHA: All 72 Plates from "Documents Decoratifs" in Original Color, Alphonse Mucha. Rare copyright-free design portfolio by high priest of Art Nouveau. Jewelry, wallpaper, stained glass, furniture, figure studies, plant and animal motifs, etc. Only complete one-volume edition. 80pp. 9⅜ × 12¼. 24044-4 Pa. $9.95

ANIMALS: 1,419 COPYRIGHT-FREE ILLUSTRATIONS OF MAMMALS, BIRDS, FISH, INSECTS, ETC., edited by Jim Harter. Clear wood engravings present, in extremely lifelike poses, over 1,000 species of animals. One of the most extensive pictorial sourcebooks of its kind. Captions. Index. 284pp. 9 × 12. 23766-4 Pa. $9.95

OBELISTS FLY HIGH, C. Daly King. Masterpiece of American detective fiction, long out of print, involves murder on a 1935 transcontinental flight—"a very thrilling story"—NY Times. Unabridged and unaltered republication of the edition published by William Collins Sons & Co. Ltd., London, 1935. 288pp. 5⅜ × 8½. (Available in U.S. only) 25036-9 Pa. $5.95

VICTORIAN AND EDWARDIAN FASHION: A Photographic Survey, Alison Gernsheim. First fashion history completely illustrated by contemporary photographs. Full text plus 235 photos, 1840-1914, in which many celebrities appear. 240pp. 6½ × 9¼. 24205-6 Pa. $6.95

THE ART OF THE FRENCH ILLUSTRATED BOOK, 1700-1914, Gordon N. Ray. Over 630 superb book illustrations by Fragonard, Delacroix, Daumier, Doré, Grandville, Manet, Mucha, Steinlen, Toulouse-Lautrec and many others. Preface. Introduction. 633 halftones. Indices of artists, authors & titles, binders and provenances. Appendices. Bibliography. 608pp. 8⅜ × 11¼. 25086-5 Pa. $24.95

THE WONDERFUL WIZARD OF OZ, L. Frank Baum. Facsimile in full color of America's finest children's classic. 143 illustrations by W. W. Denslow. 267pp. 5⅜ × 8½. 20691-2 Pa. $7.95

FRONTIERS OF MODERN PHYSICS: New Perspectives on Cosmology, Relativity, Black Holes and Extraterrestrial Intelligence, Tony Rothman, et al. For the intelligent layman. Subjects include: cosmological models of the universe; black holes; the neutrino; the search for extraterrestrial intelligence. Introduction. 46 black-and-white illustrations. 192pp. 5⅜ × 8½. 24587-X Pa. $7.95

THE FRIENDLY STARS, Martha Evans Martin & Donald Howard Menzel. Classic text marshalls the stars together in an engaging, non-technical survey, presenting them as sources of beauty in night sky. 23 illustrations. Foreword. 2 star charts. Index. 147pp. 5⅜ × 8½. 21099-5 Pa. $3.95

FADS AND FALLACIES IN THE NAME OF SCIENCE, Martin Gardner. Fair, witty appraisal of cranks, quacks, and quackeries of science and pseudoscience: hollow earth, Velikovsky, orgone energy, Dianetics, flying saucers, Bridey Murphy, food and medical fads, etc. Revised, expanded In the Name of Science. "A very able and even-tempered presentation."—The New Yorker. 363pp. 5⅜ × 8. 20394-8 Pa. $6.95

ANCIENT EGYPT: ITS CULTURE AND HISTORY, J. E Manchip White. From pre-dynastics through Ptolemies: society, history, political structure, religion, daily life, literature, cultural heritage. 48 plates. 217pp. 5⅜ × 8½. 22548-8 Pa. $5.95

SIR HARRY HOTSPUR OF HUMBLETHWAITE, Anthony Trollope. Incisive, unconventional psychological study of a conflict between a wealthy baronet, his idealistic daughter, and their scapegrace cousin. The 1870 novel in its first inexpensive edition in years. 250pp. 5⅜ × 8½. 24953-0 Pa. $5.95

LASERS AND HOLOGRAPHY, Winston E. Kock. Sound introduction to burgeoning field, expanded (1981) for second edition. Wave patterns, coherence, lasers, diffraction, zone plates, properties of holograms, recent advances. 84 illustrations. 160pp. 5⅜ × 8¼. (Except in United Kingdom) 24041-X Pa. $3.95

INTRODUCTION TO ARTIFICIAL INTELLIGENCE: SECOND, EN-LARGED EDITION, Philip C. Jackson, Jr. Comprehensive survey of artificial intelligence—the study of how machines (computers) can be made to act intelligently. Includes introductory and advanced material. Extensive notes updating the main text. 132 black-and-white illustrations. 512pp. 5⅜ × 8½. 24864-X Pa. $8.95

HISTORY OF INDIAN AND INDONESIAN ART, Ananda K. Coomaraswamy. Over 400 illustrations illuminate classic study of Indian art from earliest Harappa finds to early 20th century. Provides philosophical, religious and social insights. 304pp. 6⅜ × 9⅜. 25005-9 Pa. $9.95

THE GOLEM, Gustav Meyrink. Most famous supernatural novel in modern European literature, set in Ghetto of Old Prague around 1890. Compelling story of mystical experiences, strange transformations, profound terror. 13 black-and-white illustrations. 224pp. 5⅜ × 8½. (Available in U.S. only) 25025-3 Pa. $6.95

ARMADALE, Wilkie Collins. Third great mystery novel by the author of *The Woman in White* and *The Moonstone*. Original magazine version with 40 illustrations. 597pp. 5⅜ × 8½. 23429-0 Pa. $9.95

PICTORIAL ENCYCLOPEDIA OF HISTORIC ARCHITECTURAL PLANS, DETAILS AND ELEMENTS: With 1,880 Line Drawings of Arches, Domes, Doorways, Facades, Gables, Windows, etc., John Theodore Haneman. Sourcebook of inspiration for architects, designers, others. Bibliography. Captions. 141pp. 9 × 12. 24605-1 Pa. $7.95

BENCHLEY LOST AND FOUND, Robert Benchley. Finest humor from early 30's, about pet peeves, child psychologists, post office and others. Mostly unavailable elsewhere. 73 illustrations by Peter Arno and others. 183pp. 5⅜ × 8½.
22410-4 Pa. $4.95

ERTÉ GRAPHICS, Erté. Collection of striking color graphics: *Seasons, Alphabet, Numerals, Aces* and *Precious Stones*. 50 plates, including 4 on covers. 48pp. 9⅜ × 12¼. 23580-7 Pa. $6.95

THE JOURNAL OF HENRY D. THOREAU, edited by Bradford Torrey, F. H. Allen. Complete reprinting of 14 volumes, 1837–61, over two million words; the sourcebooks for *Walden*, etc. Definitive. All original sketches, plus 75 photographs. 1,804pp. 8½ × 12¼. 20312-3, 20313-1 Cloth., Two-vol. set $120.00

CASTLES: THEIR CONSTRUCTION AND HISTORY, Sidney Toy. Traces castle development from ancient roots. Nearly 200 photographs and drawings illustrate moats, keeps, baileys, many other features. Caernarvon, Dover Castles, Hadrian's Wall, Tower of London, dozens more. 256pp. 5⅜ × 8¼.
24898-4 Pa. $6.95

AMERICAN CLIPPER SHIPS: 1833–1858, Octavius T. Howe & Frederick C. Matthews. Fully-illustrated, encyclopedic review of 352 clipper ships from the period of America's greatest maritime supremacy. Introduction. 109 halftones. 5 black-and-white line illustrations. Index. Total of 928pp. 5⅜ × 8½.
25115-2, 25116-0 Pa., Two-vol. set $17.90

TOWARDS A NEW ARCHITECTURE, Le Corbusier. Pioneering manifesto by great architect, near legendary founder of "International School." Technical and aesthetic theories, views on industry, economics, relation of form to function, "mass-production spirit," much more. Profusely illustrated. Unabridged translation of 13th French edition. Introduction by Frederick Etchells. 320pp. 6⅛ × 9¼. (Available in U.S. only)
25023-7 Pa. $8.95

THE BOOK OF KELLS, edited by Blanche Cirker. Inexpensive collection of 32 full-color, full-page plates from the greatest illuminated manuscript of the Middle Ages, painstakingly reproduced from rare facsimile edition. Publisher's Note. Captions. 32pp. 9⅜ × 12¼.
24345-1 Pa. $4.95

BEST SCIENCE FICTION STORIES OF H. G. WELLS, H. G. Wells. Full novel *The Invisible Man*, plus 17 short stories: "The Crystal Egg," "Aepyornis Island," "The Strange Orchid," etc. 303pp. 5⅜ × 8½. (Available in U.S. only)
21531-8 Pa. $6.95

AMERICAN SAILING SHIPS: Their Plans and History, Charles G. Davis. Photos, construction details of schooners, frigates, clippers, other sailcraft of 18th to early 20th centuries—plus entertaining discourse on design, rigging, nautical lore, much more. 137 black-and-white illustrations. 240pp. 6⅛ × 9¼.
24658-2 Pa. $6.95

ENTERTAINING MATHEMATICAL PUZZLES, Martin Gardner. Selection of author's favorite conundrums involving arithmetic, money, speed, etc., with lively commentary. Complete solutions. 112pp. 5⅜ × 8½.
25211-6 Pa. $2.95

THE WILL TO BELIEVE, HUMAN IMMORTALITY, William James. Two books bound together. Effect of irrational on logical, and arguments for human immortality. 402pp. 5⅜ × 8½.
20291-7 Pa. $7.95

THE HAUNTED MONASTERY and THE CHINESE MAZE MURDERS, Robert Van Gulik. 2 full novels by Van Gulik continue adventures of Judge Dee and his companions. An evil Taoist monastery, seemingly supernatural events; overgrown topiary maze that hides strange crimes. Set in 7th-century China. 27 illustrations. 328pp. 5⅜ × 8½.
23502-5 Pa. $6.95

CELEBRATED CASES OF JUDGE DEE (DEE GOONG AN), translated by Robert Van Gulik. Authentic 18th-century Chinese detective novel; Dee and associates solve three interlocked cases. Led to Van Gulik's own stories with same characters. Extensive introduction. 9 illustrations. 237pp. 5⅜ × 8½.
23337-5 Pa. $4.95

Prices subject to change without notice.
Available at your book dealer or write for free catalog to Dept. GI, Dover Publications, Inc., 31 East 2nd St., Mineola, N.Y. 11501. Dover publishes more than 175 books each year on science, elementary and advanced mathematics, biology, music, art, literary history, social sciences and other areas.